Catholics
in America

Religion in American Life

JON BUTLER & HARRY S. STOUT
GENERAL EDITORS

Catholics in America

James T. Fisher

OXFORD
UNIVERSITY PRESS

To Charlie

OXFORD
UNIVERSITY PRESS

Oxford   New York
Athens Auckland Bangkok Bogotá Buenos Aires Calcutta
Cape Town Chennai Dar es Salaam Delhi Florence Hong Kong Istanbul
Karachi Kuala Lumpur Madrid Melbourne Mexico City Mumbai
Nairobi Paris São Paulo Singapore Taipei Tokyo Toronto Warsaw
and associated companies in
Berlin Ibadan

Copyright © 2000 by James T. Fisher
Published by Oxford University Press, Inc.
198 Madison Avenue, New York, New York 10016
www.oup.com

Library of Congress Cataloging-in-Publication Data

Fisher, James T.
    Catholics in America / by James T. Fisher
        p. cm. — (Religion in American life)
    Includes bibliographical references and index.
    ISBN 0-19-511179-6 (library edition)
    1. Catholic Church—North America—History. I. Title. II. Series.

BX1403.2.F57   2000
282'7—dc21   00-024991

9 8 7 6 5 4 3 2 1

Printed in the United States of America
on acid-free paper

Design and layout: Loraine Machlin
Picture research: Lisa Kirchner

On the cover: Festa by Ralph Fasanella, 1957
Frontispiece: Altar servers at the Basilica of the National Shrine of the Immaculate Conception
in Washington, D.C.

Contents

Editors' Introduction

JON BUTLER & HARRY S. STOUT, GENERAL EDITORS

Catholics have trod a remarkable path from suppression and persecution in colonial and 19th-century America to exemplars of modern American religion and culture. Catholicism took root and prospered everywhere—early Maryland, the Spanish Southwest, the old Northeast, and the great Middle West. Propelled by the early English Catholics who settled Maryland; Father Junipiero Serra and his controversial missions to Native Americans; Irish immigrants fleeing Ireland's disastrous potato famine and Germans in search of farmland; Italian, Mexican, and Puerto Rican immigrants who flocked to modern America's cities; and African Americans in flight from Protestant racism—Catholicism is now the nation's single largest religion.

James Fisher's *Catholics in America* describes all the agony and achievement of the American Catholic experience across four centuries. It vividly portrays women's crucial roles in American Catholic development, from Saint Elizabeth Seton to Dorothy Day. It describes the vision and authority of the Church's powerful bishops, from John Carroll and John Ireland to Cardinal Francis Spellman. It illustrates lay Catholics' vivid interactions with American popular culture, from Finley Peter Dunne's "Mr. Dooley" to the introspective wisdom of Thomas Merton in the 1940s and the writings of "beat" author Jack Kerouac in the 1950s. Throughout, Fisher's account breathes the life and energy that Catholicism's believers have brought to America for more than 300 years.

This book is part of a unique 17-volume series that explores the evolution, character, and dynamics of religion in American life from 1500 to the end of the 20th century. As late as the 1960s, historians paid relatively little attention to religion beyond studies of New England's Puritans. But since then, American religious history and its contemporary expression have been the subject of intense inquiry. These new studies have thoroughly transformed our knowledge of almost every American religious group and have fully revised our understanding of religion's role in U.S. history.

It is impossible to capture the flavor and character of the American experience without understanding the connections between secular activities and religion. Spirituality stood at the center of Native American societies before European colonization and has continued to do so long after. Religion—and the freedom to express it—motivated millions of immigrants to come to the United States from remarkably different cultures, and the exposure to new ideas and ways of living shaped their experience. It also fueled tension among different ethnic and racial groups in America and, regretfully, accounted for difficult episodes of bigotry in American society. Religion urged Americans to expand the nation—first within the continental United States, then through overseas conquests and missionary work—and has had a profound influence on American politics, from the era of the Puritans to the present. Finally, religion contributes to the extraordinary diversity that has, for four centuries, made the United States one of the world's most dynamic societies.

The Religion in American Life series explores the historical traditions that have made religious freedom and spiritual exploration central features of American society. It emphasizes the experience of religion in America—what men and women have understood by religion, how it has affected politics and society, and how Americans have used it to shape their daily lives.

Religion in American Life

JON BUTLER & HARRY S. STOUT
GENERAL EDITORS

RELIGION IN COLONIAL AMERICA
Jon Butler

RELIGION IN NINETEENTH CENTURY AMERICA
Grant Wacker

RELIGION IN TWENTIETH CENTURY AMERICA
Randall Balmer

BUDDHISTS, HINDUS, AND SIKHS IN AMERICA
Gurinder Singh Mann, Paul David Numrich & Raymond B. Williams

CATHOLICS IN AMERICA
James T. Fisher

JEWS IN AMERICA
Hasia R. Diner

MORMONS IN AMERICA
Claudia Lauper Bushman & Richard Lyman Bushman

MUSLIMS IN AMERICA
Frederick Denny

ORTHODOX CHRISTIANS IN AMERICA
John H. Erickson

PROTESTANTS IN AMERICA
Mark A. Noll

AFRICAN-AMERICAN RELIGION
Albert J. Raboteau

ALTERNATIVE AMERICAN RELIGIONS
Stephen J. Stein

NATIVE AMERICAN RELIGION
Joel W. Martin

CHURCH AND STATE IN AMERICA
Edwin S. Gaustad

IMMIGRATION AND AMERICAN RELIGION
Jenna Weissman Joselit

WOMEN AND AMERICAN RELIGION
Ann Braude

BIOGRAPHICAL SUPPLEMENT AND SERIES INDEX
Darryl Hart & Ann Henderson Hart

Chapter 1

Catholics in the New World

O n April 14, 1528, a band of 400 Spanish explorers in four ships made landfall on the west coast of Florida, in a bay not far from the present-day city of Sarasota. The expedition was led by red-bearded Pánfilo de Narváez, a one-eyed former governor of Cuba. His second in command was 37-year-old Álvar Núñez Cabeza de Vaca, a veteran of several military campaigns on behalf of the Holy Roman Empire and the heir to a family with large landholdings near the southern Spanish coastal city of Cadiz. After being deposed as governor of Paraguay, Cabeza de Vaca would return in chains to Cadiz in 1543, the same port to which Christopher Columbus, the devoutly Catholic explorer from Genoa, had returned bound in irons following his third voyage to the New World, in 1500. Cabeza de Vaca, like Columbus, was subject to the whims of his sponsors and the resentments of his subordinates. His setbacks, however, could not diminish the magnitude of his achievement as the first European to travel across the North American continent, from Florida to the Gulf of California.

Cabeza de Vaca compiled a report of the ill-fated Florida expedition that has been described as the first great work of American literature. It is also a testimony to the author's powerful devotion to the Roman Catholic Church. The Spanish expeditionary party, which included five priests of the Franciscan order (a community founded by St. Francis of Assisi in

An engraving depicts the first encounter of Christopher Columbus and Native Americans at Hispaniola (present-day Dominican Republic). The cross, swords, and gifts indicate that religious, political, and economic interests were linked together in the Age of Exploration.

1209), was charged with conquering the Florida territory, believed at the time to extend far to the west of its location on the peninsula. Shortly after going ashore the Spaniards captured four Native Americans, whom they called Indians and who indicated through the use of sign language the existence of a gold-laden province to the northwest. In the course of seeking and later fleeing from that desolate terrain, all but four of the original explorers perished. Among the survivors was Cabeza de Vaca, who was shipwrecked off the coast of Texas and rescued by Native Americans in November 1528. He served them over the next six years as healer, slave, and merchant before fleeing with his three compatriots into the interior of New Spain, in what is today the country of Mexico.

The Spaniards came to the New World to seek riches and to claim vast expanses of land for the Crown as well as to win souls for the church. Along with the vast majority of Europeans who came to North America, Cabeza de Vaca believed that the Indians were "wild, untaught savages" who must be converted to Christianity. The idea that Native American civilizations could be considered complete and valuable in their present state was inconceivable to Catholics and Protestants alike in the age of exploration and conquest. In his report to Charles I, the king of Spain, who also ruled as Holy Roman Emperor Charles V, Cabeza de Vaca described how he and his colleagues "taught the people by signs, which they understood, that in Heaven there was a Man we called God, who had created the heavens and the earth; that all good came from Him and that we worshipped and obeyed Him and called Him our Lord; and that if they would do the same, all would be well with them." Yet just as Cabeza de Vaca recognized differences between the Native American tribes he encountered, he also learned that not all of his compatriots shared his view that the Indians "must be won by kindness, the only certain way."

Cabeza de Vaca referred to the Europeans in North America simply as Christians. Martin Luther, the German leader of a reform movement that led to a proliferation of Protestant churches in northern Europe, had been excommunicated from the Roman Catholic Church just seven years prior to the expedition led by Pánfilo de Narváez. But the Reformation was of little concern to the Spaniards, who continued to equate Christianity with the Roman Catholicism that had reigned throughout Europe for well over a thousand years.

Roman Catholics believe that Jesus was crucified, died, and was buried, and rose again on the third day as a sign that he truly was the Messiah, the only Son of God. Forty days after his resurrection Jesus ascended into heaven and took his place at the right hand of God. The third person of the Blessed Trinity, the Holy Spirit, soon directed the apostles to spread the news of Christ's life and resurrection,

through which he conquered death and offered eternal life to those who believed in him. The leader of these apostles, Peter ("You are Peter, and on this rock I will build my church," Jesus tells his disciple, as reported in the Gospel of Matthew) eventually made his way to Rome, the center of the Western world at that time.

Peter's successors as head of the church, the bishops of Rome, came to be known as the popes. The early church endured much suffering and persecution, but by the fourth century Roman Catholicism had become the dominant religious and cultural force in Europe. Through the centuries, the church inevitably became embroiled in political controversies that led to calls for reform. Martin Luther, a former priest who rose to prominence in the early 16th century, was not the first but was by far the most influential critic of certain practices within the church that were widely viewed as scandalous. In the two centuries before Luther's time the church had suffered from corrupt leadership and rampant nepotism (the granting of high positions to family members, in this case relatives of the popes). Martin Luther particularly objected to the church's selling of indulgences, spiritual favors that removed "vestiges" of sins already forgiven by God through the church. Luther insisted that God's grace was a

The Inscription Rock at New Mexico's El Moro National Monument, translated from Spanish, reads: "Here was the general Don Diego de Vargas who conquered for our faith and Royal Crown all of New Mexico at his own expense year 1692." In that year de Vargas was sent by Spain to make peace with Pueblo Indians who had driven settlers and missionaries out of the territory in 1680.

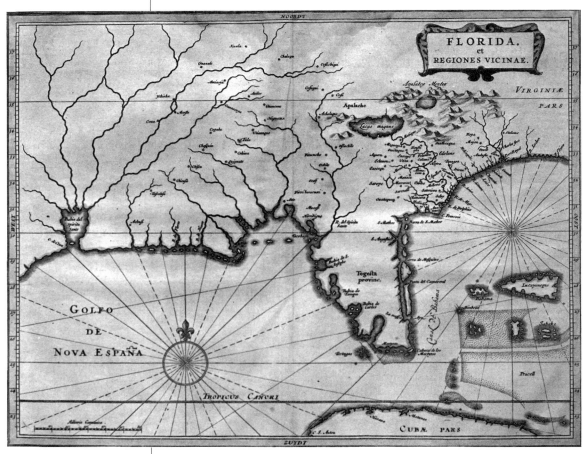

FLORIDA.
et
REGIONES VICINAE.

A 16th-century Spanish map of Florida and the region around the Gulf of New Spain (Mexico). The map was drawn several decades after the journey of Cabeza de Vaca along the Gulf Coast.

free gift not linked to such spiritual "works" as indulgences. The Protestant reform movement Luther helped launch taught that women and men were granted salvation by faith alone, not by "good works" that could be manipulated by the church's earthly leaders.

The Spanish Catholic explorers of the New World believed that in bringing Christianity to its Indians and claiming its possessions for the Crown they would earn eternal salvation. Cabeza de Vaca was not a priest, but he was no less committed than his Franciscan countrymen to the conversion and spiritual welfare of the Native Americans. Tensions unavoidably erupted among the Spaniards in North America, however, pitting those who viewed their mission as primarily religious against the many *conquistadores* (conquerors) whose motives were more personal, political, and economic in nature. Cabeza de Vaca sought to spare the Native Americans from the *conquistadores* who were killing or enslaving them. At the same time, however, he warned the Indians, as he wrote in his report to the king, that if they failed to "serve God as we required," the Christians "would treat them hard and carry them away to strange lands as slaves."

Some *conquistadores* claimed that the Native Americans should not be converted to Christianity, arguing that they were not even human. In response, in 1537 Pope Paul III issued a papal decree in which he affirmed that "the Indians are truly men" who "are by no means to be deprived of their liberty or the possession of their property; even though they be outside the faith of Jesus Christ; and that they may and should, freely and legitimately, enjoy their liberty and the possession of their property; nor should they be in any way enslaved." But a year later, Holy Roman Emperor Charles V—who in his other capacity as the king of Spain was also the sponsor of Cabeza de Vaca's mission—convinced the pope to revoke punishments imposed by missionaries on *conquistadores* who had mistreated Indians. Although Charles subsequently instituted reforms designed to lessen the abuse of Native Americans by Spaniards in the New World, irreparable harm had already been done.

Cabeza de Vaca's journey helped pave the way for the rapid expansion of Roman Catholicism in the regions he explored. On September 8, 1565, a solemn mass was celebrated at St. Augustine, Florida, on the feast day of the nativity of the Blessed Virgin Mary. The ceremony also marked the arrival of Pedro Menendez de Avilés, captain-general of the Indies fleet, who had been dispatched by King Philip II of Spain to establish a permanent Catholic settlement in Florida. St. Augustine became the site of the first American parish. Mission stations were soon established in nearby villages by Franciscans as well as by Jesuits, members of a religious order (the Society of Jesus) founded by Ignatius Loyola and formally established by the church in

In September 1565 the Spanish explorer Pedro Menendez de Aviles established a settlement near a harbor on the northeast coast of Florida and named it San Augustin (St. Augustine). Four Spanish priests accompanying Menendez began a mission to the Timucan Indians who inhabited the site.

This painting in the cathedral at St. Augustine depicts the first mass celebrated at the settlement, on February 8, 1565. The oldest American parish was also established on the site.

1540. A former soldier from the Basque region of present-day Spain, Ignatius developed a spiritual doctrine that stressed the integration of prayer and service: Jesuits were urged to "find God in all things."

Spanish Catholicism of the Franciscan and Jesuit varieties exerted great impact on the missions created between the early 17th and late 18th centuries in present-day Texas, Arizona, New Mexico, and California. Because Mexico City was the capital of New Spain, these remote northern outposts were often sparsely populated and many were short-lived, but they left a complex legacy among the Native American populations for many generations to come.

The missions were a central component of both the church's activity in the New World and the highly elaborate imperial bureaucracy orchestrated from Spain. The missions were designed to gather local Indians together in one place so that, as Pope Paul III commanded in 1537, they "should be converted to the faith of Jesus Christ by preaching the word of

God and by the example of good and holy living." Far more than mere centers of conversion and worship, the missions also provided educational, medical, and social services. The Spanish hoped to transplant a piece of their civilization to the frontier and build a self-sustaining community that would separate converted Indians from the non-Christians living outside the walls of the mission.

The Indians were enticed by the spiritual and healing prowess of the missionaries as well as by the promise of protection and the offer of such basic necessities as food and shelter. As a Jesuit in Arizona explained, "Indians do not come to Christian service when they do not see the maize pot boiling." At the same time, many Indians were attracted to the richly symbolic nature of the Roman Catholic faith. As a priest at the mission in San Francisco recalled, "I brought out a representation of our holy father St. Francis, most edifying, and upon my presenting it to the Indians to kiss they did so with much veneration, to all appearances, and willingness, that they stole my heart and the hearts of all who observed them."

An Italian Jesuit, Francisco Eusebio Kino, founded Spanish missions across southern Arizona in the 1690s. In 1700 he established the mission of San Xavier del Bac on a site near contemporary Tucson. The church Kino built there was destroyed, but another mission church was erected in the last two decades of the 18th century. The church of San Xavier del Bac (known as "the White Dove of the Desert" for its graceful appearance) is a blend of baroque, Moorish, and Byzantine styles and is widely considered the finest example of Spanish Renaissance architecture found in America. Kino worked among the Pima Indians and was more respectful of Native American cultures than many of his missionary colleagues were. In an account of his work, written in 1710, Kino described

The interior of the church of San Xavier del Bac, near Tucson, Arizona, displays 150 carefully arranged images of Jesus, Mary, saints, and angels.

his travels in the Southwest and reported that over a 21-year period "there have been brought to our friendship and to the desire of receiving our holy Catholic faith . . . more than thirty thousand souls, there being sixteen thousand of Pimas alone."

The California missions founded by the Spanish Franciscan Junipero Serra between 1769 and his death in 1784 were noted for their ambitious and often lucrative agricultural programs. Serra was a former philosophy teacher who was working as a missionary in Mexico when, at the age of 59, he was appointed to launch the Franciscans' California mission program. He quickly established communities at San Diego, San Luis Obispo, San Francisco, and other locations along the California coast. Serra's motto was "always forward, never back," and he proved an able builder and administrator of missions.

The California missions, like those in the desert Southwest, offered their subjects protection against both rival Native Americans and violent elements within the community of Spanish settlers. The mission *padres* (Spanish for "fathers") insisted that the Indians under their care convert willingly, but these "neophytes," or newly converted people, were not permitted to leave the missions for extended periods, in part because the padres took full responsibility for the souls of their converts. The inhabitants of the missions were often severely punished if they attempted to leave, and even after converting to Christianity they had few of the rights and privileges enjoyed by the Spaniards. Between 1769 and 1784 more than 6,000 California Indians were baptized at missions founded by Serra. For several decades after his death, California was dependent for its survival on the economic productivity of the missions he had set up.

The Spanish missions in North America differed from one another in certain respects but shared many features in common. The missionaries directed much of their efforts toward Native American children, through whom they hoped to create new generations of Christians. In fact, the missionaries tended to treat all the Native Americans as children who could only gradually embrace the European Christian way of life; in the meantime they would remain separated from both the Spaniards and other Indians outside the enclosure. This segregation did not, however, prevent the spread of diseases among the native populations, who lacked immunity to many sicknesses, such as cholera and smallpox, introduced to North America by Europeans. The combination of disease, mistreatment, and overwork had a devastating impact on Native American populations throughout the Southwest.

While some of the earliest Franciscan and Jesuit missionaries had a sincere desire to understand the Native Americans' languages and cultures, the Spanish government quickly discouraged these efforts for fear the missionaries would shift their loyalties from the Crown to their Indian subjects. Although Catholicism was the official state religion in Spain, the church had allowed itself to become dominated by the monarchy, which therefore enjoyed full control over the religious institutions established in North America.

The Spanish conquerors found themselves beset by internal strife, especially between missionaries and colonial administrators. In 1773 Father Serra traveled to Mexico to petition the colonial government successfully to free the missions from civil control. Several years later he reported that "when we came not a Christian existed here . . . we regenerated all in Christ; and . . . we have come and we are all here for their welfare and salvation. At all events, I believe it is well known that we love them." That love did not translate, however, into a belief in self-rule for their Native American Christian neophytes. The Franciscans' deeply spiritual concern for the welfare of their charges was not always sufficient to protect them against exploitation and brutality, though the plight of the Indians in California only worsened when the Mexican government removed the padres from the missions in the 1830s.

Junipero Serra and many other Spanish missionaries to North America were inspired by the religious renewal that began in 16th-century Spanish Catholicism, an era dominated by such remarkable figures as St. Teresa of Avila, St. John of the Cross, and St. Ignatius Loyola. These individuals were visionaries who inspired many others to endure hardship and suffering and to sacrifice their own desires for the good of the church.

But Spanish Catholics in North America sometimes combined this powerful quest on behalf of the church with an equally fervent drive for

French Jesuit missionaries occasionally provided illustrations along with written accounts of their work with Native Americans in New France. While intent on converting Indians, the missionaries also made note of local customs and native wildlife.

personal spiritual authority. Álvar Núñez Cabeza de Vaca, for example, had returned to New Spain in 1543 to conduct an expedition deep into the jungles of Paraguay in search of the legendary golden city of Manoa. His troops soon grew resentful of him, however, not only because he forbade them to mistreat the native peoples but also because he presented himself as a "divine agent" and ordered his men to transport his weighty camp bed across the jungle. He was deposed and returned to Spain a prisoner, then was vindicated only a few years before his death in 1557. Cabeza de Vaca's complex legacy—his blend of religious zeal and personal grandiosity—was echoed in the lives and work of numerous Europeans who sought to bring Christianity to North America in the 16th, 17th, and 18th centuries.

While the Spanish focused their colonizing efforts on the "borderlands" of Mexico, the 17th century saw the French concentrate on Canada. From that base adventurers and missionaries explored parts of the future states of Maine, New York, and Michigan, as well as the Mississippi Valley. Unlike Spain, France was home to a significant community of Protestants, known as Huguenots, who had been granted limited religious freedom under the Edict of Nantes in 1598. In 1608 the first permanent French settlement in North America was founded at Quebec by Samuel de Champlain, a devout Catholic acting as the agent of a Huguenot businessman, Pierre du Guast, Sieur de Monts. Because few Huguenots had settled in North America prior to the revocation of the Edict of Nantes in 1685, French Canada became dominated by Catholics, many of whom hoped to build a Christian society in the wilderness, while others—notably the fur traders—came seeking riches.

From the 1630s until 1763, when Canada came under British rule, the Jesuits were the dominant missionaries of New France. The Jesuit missionary Isaac Jogues worked among the Huron Indians in Michigan and northern New York, where he was captured by Iroquois rivals of the Huron in 1642. A year later Jogues escaped and made his way back to France, where the visible evidence of his tortures in New France generated widespread acclaim for his sacrificial work. Like many French

Catholics of the period, Father Jogues pursued "mortifications," or ritual practices of self-denial, in the name of the church. It was believed that through suffering one not only grew closer to Christ, who had died on the cross, but became as well a purified vehicle for God's saving grace in the world. In 1643 Jogues explained to his Jesuit superior that he did not attempt to flee the Iroquois in the early stages of his captivity, because "on this cross, to which our Lord has nailed me beside himself, am I resolved by his grace to live and die." Isaac Jogues eagerly returned to New France in 1644, only to be killed while attempting to convert the Iroquois northwest of Albany, New York.

Although Father Jogues was among eight slain missionaries later canonized as the North American Martyrs, the French were somewhat more successful in their relationships with the Native Americans than the Spanish were. The Jesuits' annual reports to their superiors, excerpts of which were published in a yearly missionary journal known as the *Relations*, demonstrated an impressive understanding of tribal customs and languages as well as occasional anger directed at French fur traders whose "avarice," as a Jesuit complained in 1634, had earned the "contempt" of the native population. As Jean de Brébeuf, another of the North American Martyrs, explained to his colleagues in 1637, "You must have sincere affection for the Savages, looking upon them as ransomed by the blood of the Son of God, and as our brethren with whom we are to pass the rest of our lives."

The missionaries clearly believed that their primary goal was to Christianize the Native Americans. In central New York they attracted approximately 2,000 converts beginning in the 1660s. The most notable among these was a young woman named Tekakwitha, who was born in 1656 in the upstate New York Mohawk village of Ossernenon to an Iroquois father and a Christian Algonquin mother. Both parents died when Tekakwitha was four years old, during a smallpox epidemic that greatly weakened the child and left her disfigured and nearly blind. Tekakwitha was raised by an aunt and by an uncle who was the chief authority in the village. As a child she had some contact with missionaries but it was in

Born 1607. Died 1646.

The French Jesuit missionary and martyr Isaac Jogues is commemorated in a 1904 illustration. The Latin phrase *Ad Majorem Dei Gloriam* ("For the Greater Glory of God") is the unofficial motto of the Society of Jesus, or Jesuits.

her early adulthood, after rejecting a proposed marriage, that she was converted by the Jesuit missionary James de Lamberville in 1676 and adopted the Christian name Kateri.

Kateri Tekakwitha was described by another Jesuit as "a soul filled with the most precious gifts of heaven," but when she declared to her family that she could no longer work in the fields on Sundays she was punished so severely that she fled the village for refuge at the home near Montreal of an adopted sister who had also become a Christian. Kateri became so devoted to helping the sick and delivering firewood to the poor that one Jesuit called her an angel of charity. Kateri, her close companion Marie-Therese Tegaiaguenta, and several other Native American convert women formed a group they called the Slavery of the Blessed Virgin. This small community blended Iroquois and Catholic spiritual practices, fasting for long intervals and enduring exposure to the cold in a self-sacrificial quest. Kateri was so determined to imitate the life and sufferings of Christ that she neglected her own health and died in 1680 at the age of 24.

In 1980 the church beatified—declared to be among the blessed in heaven—Kateri Tekakwitha, in a prelude to her possible elevation to sainthood. Although "the Lily of the Mohawks" was clearly an exceptional convert, Kateri's estrangement from her own community helps explain why the French missionaries, while more sensitive than were the Spanish to Indian customs, were not particularly successful in North America. Christianity took permanent root among the Native Americans only when it adapted itself to their own way of life in a permanent community setting.

From an American perspective, perhaps the most enduring accomplishment of the Jesuits was their role in the exploration of vast territories to the southwest of New France. The most renowned of the missionary explorers, Jacques Marquette, accompanied the Quebec-born adventurer

Louis Jolliet in 1673 on a journey by canoe from St. Ignace in the Upper Peninsula of Michigan across Lake Michigan and down the Fox and Wisconsin rivers to the Mississippi, which they joined just below the present-day town of Prairie du Chien, Wisconsin. One week into their journey down that heartland river, they observed some footprints that they followed to a village of Illinois Indians, who warmly greeted Jolliet and the Jesuit "Blackrobe" and took them to the village of "the Great Captain of all the Illinois."

According to his report of this encounter, Marquette promptly informed an assemblage there that he had been sent by God on a peaceful mission because He "wished to make himself Known to all the peoples" and that it was up to the Illinois "to acknowledge and obey Him." When the Native American captain urged the French party to stay rather than risk their lives in the wilderness, Marquette said he "replied that I Feared not death, and that I regarded no happiness greater than that of losing my life for the glory of Him who has made all." Marquette would die of dysentery in Michigan in 1675 as he neared the end of a second, shorter journey into the Illinois country. The 1673 trip with Jolliet, however, took the men far into the heart of the Mississippi Valley, below the confluence of the Ohio and Mississippi Rivers and into the delta region as far as present-day Arkansas. The sights they enjoyed along the way "inspired awe" in the explorers as they would in subsequent travelers down the majestic river.

The Frenchmen might have reached the Gulf of Mexico had they not feared encountering Spaniards and their Native American allies in the Louisiana Territory. By the 1670s, however, Spain's influence in what was to become the United States had already begun to decline. The French continued to expand their colonial holdings, especially in the Mississippi Valley, but they now faced a much more formidable foe than Spain. The rising British Empire had designs on North America that not only changed the political and diplomatic landscape of the New World but introduced a dramatic new religious component as well. Long before the advent of American independence, English Protestants became the dominant power in the new civilization.

Jacques Marquette's Journey Up the Mississippi River

On May 17, 1763, the French Jesuit missionary Jacques Marquette and the French-Canadian adventurer Louis Jolliet launched an expedition to explore the Mississippi Valley. They discovered a system of navigable waterways with enormous potential to support future patterns of trade and settlement. Marquette described the return stage of the voyage in his journal.

After a month's Navigation, while descending Missisipi from the 42nd to the 34th degree, and beyond, and after preaching the Gospel as well as I could to the Nations that I met, we start on the 17th of July from the village of the akensea [a Native-American community they encountered along the Mississippi, just north of the mouth of the Arkansas River], to retrace our steps. We therefore reascend the Missisipi which gives us much trouble in breasting its Currents. It is true that we leave it, at about the 38th degree, to enter another river [the Illinois], which greatly shortens our road, and takes us with but little effort to the lake of the Illinois.

We have seen nothing like this river that we enter, as regards its fertility of soil, its prairies and woods; its cattle. . . . We found on it a village of Illinois called Kaskaskia, consisting of 74 Cabins. They received us very well, and obliged me to promise that I would return to instruct them. One of the chiefs of this nation, with his young men, escorted us to the Lake of the Illinois, whence, at last, at The end of September, we reached the bay des puantz [Green Bay, Wisconsin], from which we had started at the beginning of June.

Had this voyage resulted in the salvation of even one soul, I would consider all my troubles well rewarded, and I have reason to presume that such is the case. For, when I was returning, we passed through the Illinois of Peouarea, [now Peoria] and during three days I preached the faith in all their Cabins; after which, while we were embarking, a dying child was brought to me at The water's edge, and I baptized it shortly before it died, through an admirable act of providence for the salvation of that Innocent soul.

In the British colonies of North America, Catholics represented only a tiny fraction of the population, never accounting for more than 1 percent of the total. In colonial New England particularly there were precious few Catholics to be found. In the more religiously diverse middle colonies, from New York to Maryland, a few Catholics rose to positions of prominence. The Duke of York appointed Thomas Dongan of Kildare, Ireland, governor of the New York colony in 1683. After arriving in New York, Dongan—who was one of a very small number of Catholics in the colony—made the revealing observation that not only was New York religiously diverse but most of its citizens belonged to no church of any kind. Dongan's tenure was marked by the adoption of a "Charter of Libertys and Privileges" that established religious freedom in the colony. Governor Dongan's main concerns were political and territorial: he aggressively defended New York's northern borders with French Canada and even urged Iroquois chiefs at Albany to rebuff French missionaries in the territory.

Dongan relinquished his post in August 1688, in part because his plan to replace the French missionaries in New York with British Jesuits undermined the desire of his patron, the Catholic King James II of England (the former Duke of York), for good relations with King Louis XIV of France. After King James was overthrown at the end of that year, a new, robustly anti-Catholic regime issued arrest warrants for all suspected "papists" in New York. Dongan was pursued for more than a year before he finally made his way back to England. Before long, nearly all of the Catholics in New York had taken refuge in more hospitable colonies, especially Pennsylvania, whose Quaker founders tolerated members of different faiths, though Catholics were still excluded from holding public office.

The experience of Catholics in colonial Maryland suggests that members of their faith fared better in Protestant English America during times when religious fervor was at a low ebb, as it was in Thomas Dongan's heyday. Maryland, settled in 1634 by Sir Cecil Calvert, Lord Baltimore, the son of a prominent British convert to Catholicism, provided a notable exception to the Protestant origins of the British colonies. Not even in Maryland, however, did Catholics come close to making up a majority of

Cecil Calvert founded the Maryland colony at the age of 28, after inheriting the titles and estates of his wealthy English father, the first Lord Baltimore. Calvert survived religious and political controversies in Maryland and remained the dominant figure in the colony until his death in 1675.

the population. Three Jesuit priests accompanied the first party to settle at St. Mary's, Maryland—where they established the first Catholic place of worship in the English colonies—but despite this greater presence, Lord Baltimore urged that all "acts of Roman Catholic worship" be conducted "as privately as may be" so as not to arouse the ire of local Protestants.

In the winter of 1644–45 an armed ship, *The Reformation,* brought to Maryland a group of English Puritans, who promptly seized control of the colony. Puritans were zealous Protestants determined to eliminate all remnants of "popery," or Catholic practice, in England as well as in her colonies. Between 1644 and 1646 (a period known to Maryland Catholics as the "plundering time"), several priests were arrested and banished from the colony, including the prominent Jesuit Richard White, known as the Apostle of Maryland for his pioneering service to the colony.

The Calverts regained control of Maryland late in 1646. Partly in response to the upheavals of the "plundering time," they encouraged the passage in 1649 of the Act Concerning Religion (commonly called the Act of Religious Toleration), which formally established limited religious freedom in the colony. Like many colonial proprietors, the Calverts were more concerned with the peace and prosperity of their enterprise than with promoting a uniformity of religious practice. The Act of Religious Toleration made denial of the Trinity (the belief that God is three persons in one: the Father, the Son, and the Holy Spirit) punishable by death, but it also mandated that "noe person or persons whatsoever within this Province . . . professing to believe in Jesus Christ, shall from henceforth bee any waies troubled, Molested or discountenanced for or in respect of his or her religion nor in the free exercise thereof . . . nor anyway compelled to the belief or exercise of any other Religion against his or her consent."

In its early days there was little organized religious activity of any kind to be found in Maryland. In 1654, however, Puritan zealots repealed the Act of Religious Toleration and ushered in an era of intolerance toward Catholics that would persist until the American Revolution. The Calverts were overthrown in 1689 after James II lost his throne in England, and in 1702 the Church of England was made the official state religion of Maryland. Many of the colony's elite Catholic families maintained their Catholic identity, however, and some, like the Carrolls, went on to play an important role in founding the United States of America.

The Maryland experiment proved to be highly significant for the fate of Catholics in a Protestant society. It highlighted both the possibilities and the limits of interaction between members of rival religious communities. In Maryland the suppression of Catholicism was harsh and occasionally violent, but the anti-Catholicism there was expressed much more often in words than in deeds. In 1704, for example, a Protestant governor of Maryland condemned the Catholic Mass and the teachings of the Church as "gawdy shows and serpentine policy," a hostile reference to the church's intricate body of teachings. The governor warned an American-born priest who hoped to celebrate Mass in St. Mary's City that "if you intend to live here let me hear no more of these things for if I do and they are made good against you I'll chastise you." Yet Catholics continued to gather together in private chapels for Mass as they had done since the colony's earliest days.

The Mass and the sacrament of the Eucharist form the core of the Roman Catholic faith. At Mass, the community of faith gathers together in worship ("For where two or three of them are gathered together in my name, there I am in the midst of them," Jesus told his disciples, as reported in the Gospel of Matthew). The official *Catechism of the Catholic Church* defines sacraments as "efficacious signs of grace, instituted by Christ and entrusted to the Church, by which divine life is dispensed to us." There are seven sacraments—the Eucharist, Baptism, Confirmation, Reconciliation (Penance), Anointing the Sick, Marriage, and Holy Orders—but the most central to Catholic worship is the Eucharist,

American folk artist Jack Savitsky painted *The Last Supper* in 1974. Jesus is at the center of the group, surrounded by his 12 apostles. Each has his own cup of wine and piece of bread.

described by the church as "the source and summit of the Christian life." The Eucharist, or the sacrament of Holy Communion, originated at the Last Supper, when Jesus told his apostles, as he broke bread, "This is my body which is given for you. Do this in remembrance of me." He then took a cup of wine, saying, "This cup which is poured out for you is the New Covenant in my blood."

Roman Catholics believe that during Mass, when the priest says the eucharistic prayer "consecrating" the bread and wine, "there takes place a change in the whole substance of the bread into the substance of the body of Christ our Lord and of the whole substance of the wine into the substance of his blood." Through this process, known as transubstantiation, "Christ, God and man, makes himself wholly and entirely present." The sacrament of Holy Communion produces an intimate union between the recipient and Jesus Christ and also strengthens the unity of the church, the "Mystical Body of Christ" through which all the faithful are linked to each other through Christ.

The Eucharist is a sacred mystery that cannot be fully understood through the faculty of human reason. The Maryland governor who condemned the "gawdy shows" of the Mass in 1704 was invoking a Protestant desire to simplify Christian worship by minimizing or eliminating the "mysterious" aspects of the Catholic Mass such as the use of incense, sacred images, and ornate vestments. Where the Catholic Mass of that era featured a priest intoning the sacred liturgy (the official prayers of the church used in worship) in Latin—facing not the congregation but the altar, on which he consecrated the bread and wine— Protestant services focused much more on Scripture readings and original sermons delivered by the minister. The religious differences separating these Christian faiths were significant, but political conflicts rooted in Europe also played a large role in the colonies. When Maryland's Protestants enacted laws against Catholic worship, they were settling old scores as well as indicating their continued hostility to "popery."

The laws barring public Catholicism in Maryland did not lead to wholesale conversions to Protestantism (though some prominent Catholics did convert), but rather to a kind of "tribal" sense of Catholic identity that bound the community closer together. In Maryland the Catholics tended to be more affluent than the Protestants, because many were connected to the founding families of the colony. In later years and in other places, long after the last ordinances restricting their religious freedom had been struck down, less prosperous Catholics would often echo the Maryland experience in creating closely knit communities that stood apart from the Protestant majority.

In the decades leading to the American Revolution, the anti-Catholic language that was so familiar in England and her colonies was expanded and transformed. Where New England's Puritan ministers had promoted a view of the Church of Rome as the

Kneeling congregants receive communion in the late 1950s. The archbishop in the center holds a ciborium containing consecrated hosts: the Body of Christ.

embodiment of evil, American critics of Britain's arbitrary and tyrannical rule over the colonies now condemned the king with a gusto usually reserved for attacks on the pope. With such a small number of Catholics in the colonies, however, the shifting battle of words preceding the Revolution had little impact on their daily lives.

When the Revolution began in 1776, the Catholic population of the 13 colonies was estimated at 25,000 in a total population of 2.5 million. Many Catholics supported the patriot cause, and a few contributed greatly to the struggle for independence from England. Charles Carroll, a wealthy landowner from Maryland, became an outspoken opponent of unfair colonial taxation in the early 1770s. Under the name "First Citizen," he published a series of letters in the *Maryland Gazette* arguing that taxes levied without the consent of the people's representatives were illegitimate. Carroll, who was called by one advocate of independence "a most flaming patriot," attended the First Continental Congress in Philadelphia, was a delegate to the Continental Congress two years later (where he signed the Declaration of Independence) and later helped write a new constitution for Maryland that ended discrimination against Catholics. The work of Carroll and others—including John Barry, the Irish-born "father of the American Navy," who commanded the first battleship commissioned by the Continental Congress—led George Washington to proclaim that American Catholics played their "patriotic part" in helping the colonies achieve their independence.

A Canadian-born priest, Pierre Gibault, emerged as a hero of the Revolution's western campaign. In 1768 Gibault arrived at the French missionary settlement at Kaskaskia, Illinois, the oldest of a series of communities created along the Mississippi River in the century after the Marquette-Jolliet expedition. England had acquired these French possessions in 1763, following its triumph in the Seven Years' War (or French and Indian War, as it was known in North America). Many French settlers then simply moved across the Mississippi River, to such communities as Ste. Genevieve or the new settlement of St. Louis. Gibault worked among the remaining French settlers and Native American tribes in a territory that stretched all the way to Vincennes, Indiana, on the eastern border with Illinois, whose Catholic residents had endured seven years without the services of a priest when he arrived in 1770.

When Colonel George Rogers Clark and his Virginia militiamen captured the unprotected town of Kaskaskia on July 4, 1778, Gibault led a delegation of citizens that met with Clark and pledged their support of the American government after receiving a promise of protection and freedom of religion. Father Gibault then agreed to travel to Vincennes, where he persuaded the townspeople to avoid bloodshed by taking an oath of allegiance to the new United States government. The Catholic bishop of Quebec had demanded that all French Canadians support the British, but Gibault and the French inhabitants of Vincennes had already become, in the priest's words, "good Americans." Gibault also helped persuade Native American tribes in the Illinois territory to acknowledge the new American rulers of the region.

Just as Clark had promised, the French Catholics of the Mississippi Valley and all American Catholics were guaranteed full religious freedom in the new nation that emerged from the Revolution, though Gibault and his flock would face continuing hardships on the frontier and would be exploited by American soldiers who remained in the area. Estranged both from his religious superiors and from the Americans in the Illinois territory, in 1793 Gibault moved across the Mississippi River to the settlement of New Madrid, Missouri, which was then under Spanish control. He died there in 1802. Father Pierre Gibault provided a crucial link between the French missions of the 18th century and the American Catholic community of the following century. Those who came after him would face the challenge of defining for themselves just what it meant to be Catholics in America.

Father Pierre Gibault was known as the "Patriot Priest of the West" for his support of American independence from Great Britain.

Painted by J. Wood.

Engraved by W.S. Leney, F.S.A.
& B. Tanner, F.S.A.

Reverendissimus

JOANNES CARROLL, S.T.D.

ARCHIEPISCOPUS BALTIMORIENSIS PRIMUS.

The Most Reverend

JOHN CARROLL, D.D.

FIRST ARCHBISHOP OF BALTIMORE.

Chapter 2

Building an American Catholic Community

On April 30, 1789, on the balcony of New York City's Federal Hall, General George Washington was inaugurated the first President of the United States. Several weeks later, at Whitemarsh Plantation in Maryland, John Carroll was elected the first American bishop of the Roman Catholic Church. Carroll was elected by his peers in the American priesthood, who numbered fewer than 30 in active service at the time. Many, like Carroll himself, were Jesuits who had been serving in a freelance capacity since the suppression of their order in 1773 by Pope Clement XIV, who had feared the Jesuits' growing international influence. In 1784 Pope Pius VI, with the urging of U.S. Minister to France Benjamin Franklin, named Carroll the Prefect Apostolic, or chief administrator of the church in the United States. In 1788 the pope granted a request of the U.S. clergy that they be empowered to choose their first bishop. John Carroll's election as bishop in 1789 confirmed his stature as the most revered and influential leader of Catholics living in the new American nation.

Carroll's "see," or center of authority, was in Baltimore, from which he presided over a diocese (the district under a bishop's supervision) spanning the entire country. While slightly more than half of the nation's 30,000 Catholics resided in Maryland, the remainder were distributed throughout the nation, with significant communities found in the Philadelphia area as well as in rural Kentucky, where frontier Catholics

An 1812 engraving of Bishop John Carroll, the first American Roman Catholic bishop, in clerical robes.

were served by several highly energetic French missionary priests. Like his distant cousin Charles Carroll of Carrollton, a signer of the Declaration of Independence, the new bishop had been educated in Europe in the pre-revolutionary era, where he was introduced to the Enlightenment notion of egalitarianism, the idea that all men and women are created equal. While the anticlericalism (hostility to priestly authority) of the French Revolution posed a grave threat to the church in Europe, Carroll was certain that Catholicism could thrive under America's republican form of government, in which religious freedoms were guaranteed and the state neither aided nor hindered the activities of the church.

In 1782, prior to becoming a bishop, John Carroll told a friend that he had "contracted the language of a republican." Republicanism is a system of government in which power resides in voting citizens, who elect representatives to legislative bodies that serve the interests of the whole community. In the 1780s and 1790s, John Carroll and other American priests encouraged a new type of American Catholic spirituality that stressed the values of reason and personal virtue, the same themes promoted by the republicans dominating the early political life of the nation.

Spirituality entails the manner in which individuals develop their relationship with God and the world God created. For Catholics, spirituality is always linked to the concept of "grace," which is God's free self-communication through the power of the Holy Spirit. Spirituality fosters an awareness of the presence of God's grace in human activity and in the world of creation. In the late 18th and early 19th centuries, when American Catholics were few in number and shared much in common with their Protestant compatriots, their spirituality tended to foster a personal relationship with Jesus and a faith in the power of reason to confirm Christian truths. A 1791 church document called on every American priest to preach Sunday sermons that "aim at both educating and correcting the listeners, and encouraging them in the quest for Christian perfection." Anthony Kohlmann, a Jesuit stationed in St. Peter's parish in New York City, preached an Easter sermon in 1809 in which he offered "authentication" of the Resurrection of Christ to "everyone capable of reasoning on a matter of fact."

(handwritten certificate of consecration in Latin, signed by Carolus Walmesley Episcopus Ramatensis Vicarius Apostolicus, Carolus Plowden Sacerdos assistens, Jacobus Porter Sacerdos assistens, C. Forrester presbyter Missionis apostolicae, and Thomas Stanley Sacerdos)

The certificate of consecration of Bishop John Carroll of Baltimore. John Carroll's 1789 election as the first American bishop was consecrated in August 1790 at a ceremony held in England and presided over by Bishop Charles Walmesley.

In 1790, at the urging of Bishop Carroll, Mathew Carey, a prominent Irish-born publisher living in Philadelphia, produced the first U.S. edition of the Douay-Rheims version of the Bible, often referred to as the Catholic Bible, because it was based on the official Latin translation of St. Jerome and differed in significant ways from translations favored by Protestants. Carey had come to the United States in 1784 after serving a jail term for his writings protesting British mistreatment of Irish Catholics. In 1785 he founded the *Pennsylvania Herald,* a newspaper known for its coverage of local politics, and later barely survived a duel with a bitter opponent of his views. He went on to marry Bridget Flahavan, with whom he had nine children. Carey's edition of the Douay-Rheims Bible enabled members of the laity (parishioners other than clergymen) to read the gospels and epistles and provided an essential source for personal reflection and meditation.

The first U.S. edition of the Douay-Rheims Bible—the "Catholic Bible"—was published in Philadelphia in 1790. The title page indicates that it was translated from the Vulgate, Saint Jerome's translation of the Bible (about A.D. 400) into the common language (Latin) of the time.

THE

HOLY BIBLE,

TRANSLATED FROM THE

LATIN VULGATE:

DILIGENTLY COMPARED WITH THE

HEBREW, GREEK, AND OTHER EDITIONS,

IN DIVERS LANGUAGES;

AND FIRST PUBLISHED BY

Georgetown College Library

THE ENGLISH COLLEGE AT DOWAY, ANNO 1609.

NEWLY REVISED, AND CORRECTED, ACCORDING TO

THE CLEMENTINE EDITION OF THE SCRIPTURES,

WITH ANNOTATIONS FOR ELUCIDATING

THE PRINCIPAL DIFFICULTIES OF HOLY WRIT.

Haurietis aquas in gaudio de fontibus Salvatoris. Isaiae xii. 3.

PHILADELPHIA:

PRINTED AND SOLD BY CAREY, STEWART, AND Co.

M.DCC.XC.

Mathew Carey and other early U.S. Catholic publishers took advantage of lax copyright laws to reproduce devotional and popular works by British authors. American Catholic religious practice was deeply influenced by English traditions. Robert Molyneux, an English-born Jesuit who came to Maryland in 1770, produced a widely used catechism—a handbook on the fundamentals of the faith—that was adapted from English bishop Richard Challoner's catechism, *A Short Abridgement of Christian*

Doctrine. Molyneux's version, which became known as the *Carroll Catechism,* in honor of America's first Catholic bishop, provided basic religious instruction to young Catholics from the era of the American Revolution until the late 19th century. This American catechism offered specific prayers that Catholics were urged to recite at different parts of the day, and included the following guide to morning prayers:

> When you are awake you must give your first thoughts to God, saying: O my God I give myself entirely to thee. When you are dressed you must kneel down and say the following prayers. O my God, I adore and love thee with all my heart: I return thee thanks for the innumerable favours and benefits which I have received from thy infinite goodness and mercy, especially for having preserved me this night. O my God, amiable above all things, I repent and am sorry for having offended thee, for thy own sake! Be pleased to grant, that I may spend this day well, and would rather die than commit any mortal sin.

The blend of English tradition and American innovation found in this catechism was encouraged by Bishop John Carroll, who supported the use of English at mass along with the more customary Latin. Carroll also advocated the election of bishops by those he termed the "older and more worthy clergy." At the parish level Carroll inherited a democratic tradition known as the trustee system, through which elected members of the laity directed the everyday affairs of their churches. The trustee system enjoyed many advantages at a time when priests were extremely scarce and many American Catholics sought, in the words of a Charleston, South Carolina, trustee, to "rear a National American Church, with liberties consonant to the spirit of Government, under which they live; yet, in due obedience in essentials to the Pontifical Hierarchy, and which will add a new and dignified column to the Vatican."

The situation of Catholics in America posed an unprecedented dilemma to the Vatican, the church's worldwide headquarters in Rome. The church's European leadership viewed America's developments with some wariness. There were, to be sure, drawbacks to the trustee system, which generally granted authority to affluent, well-connected members of the laity but offered little to poorer church members, who often sided with the clergy when conflicts arose over the authority of trustees to hire and fire parish priests. John Carroll became embroiled in several such disputes during his long tenure as head of the American church, which he served as bishop until his death in 1815 at the age of 80. Like many bishops who succeeded him, Carroll sought to balance his deep loyalty to the pope, to whom he readily deferred as the "spiritual head of the Church," with a conviction that American Catholics must chart their own unique course. After 1790, as Rome sought to impose the familiar European model of authority on the American church, Bishop Carroll grew more conservative and halted such innovations as the English-language liturgy.

John Carroll and his relatives Charles and Daniel Carroll were prominent members of the small American-born contingent of Roman Catholics found in Maryland and the mid-Atlantic states during the early period of the American nation. The social profile of such figures scarcely differed from that of many leading Protestants of the era. Unlike the colonial days, in the early republic there was substantial intermarriage among elite Catholics and Protestants, and shifts in religious affiliation were common. At the same time, many European priests played a key role in the American church between 1790 and 1840. They viewed themselves not as immigrants but as missionaries—with good reason, since the Vatican would officially continue to view the distant United States as "mission territory" until 1908.

In the early decades of the 19th century, tensions between European tradition and American innovation pervaded the life of the nation, sometimes with creative results. Among the most influential figures of the period was Elizabeth Ann Bayley Seton, the descendant of a wealthy colonial family with strong ties to the Episcopal Church (as the Anglican Church in America became known in the years following the Revolution). Elizabeth married New York merchant William Seton in 1794. They had five children, but the Setons' warm family life was shattered by the bankruptcy of William's business and then by his severe illness. In 1803 the couple, along with their eldest child, sailed for Italy in a desperate and ultimately futile bid to seek a cure for William's fatal tuberculosis.

While in Italy, Elizabeth Seton was introduced to the Catholic faith by family friends. She returned to New York in 1804 and was formally received into the church the following year. Although an attraction to the Catholic traditions of Europe is often cited as a factor in the conversion of American Protestants, Elizabeth Seton's spiritual journey was even more notable for its distinctly American character. Long before she traveled to Italy, Seton wore a Catholic crucifix (a replica of the cross on which Jesus died), believed in angels, and was attracted to the cloistered life of monasteries (the areas in monasteries and convents reserved strictly for their inhabitants are governed by a set of rules known as "cloister"). Yet as a young Episcopalian she also enjoyed Methodist hymns and Quaker meditations.

Seton cultivated her personal spirituality out of a diverse array of traditions, a common practice among Americans. Yet if becoming a Catholic did not require as great a theological leap as some might imagine, Seton's commitment to her new church threatened the loss of her privileged social position, a price she was willing to pay. In 1808 she accepted an invitation from William DuBourg, a French Sulpician priest (the Sulpicians were members of a religious community deeply involved in American missionary activities) to open a Catholic school for girls in Baltimore, the first of its kind in the United States.

Less than a year later, after taking the traditional vows of poverty, chastity, and obedience, Elizabeth Seton, now known as Mother Seton, gathered together a group of young women who shared her desire to live and work in a religious community. In 1809 Mother Seton and her children moved with this new community, the Sisters of Charity of St. Joseph, to rural Emmitsburg, Maryland, where they built a permanent headquarters for their new order. Mother Seton thrived in the highly disciplined environment of convent life. "I am so in love now with rules," she wrote to a friend, "that I see the *bit* of the bridle all gold, or the *reins* of all silk." Mother Seton soon clashed, however, with a Sulpician priest assigned as spiritual director to the Sisters of Charity, who sought to

In 1796 Elizabeth Ann Bayley Seton, age 22, sat for a formal portrait in New York. In 1808, three years after converting to Catholicism, she founded the Sisters of Charity of St. Joseph in Maryland.

Jean-Baptiste Point du Sable, an African-American fur trader, lived with his Native American wife and their two children on a large tract of land alongside Lake Michigan. When his wife died in 1800, Point du Sable moved to Missouri, but the site he had settled grew into the city of Chicago.

remove her as leader and impose a more austere regimen upon the community. The issues surrounding this power struggle were complex, but in pitting a French male cleric against an American female convert it set the tone for tensions that would beset the church in later decades.

Although Mother Seton freely embraced the spiritual discipline of convent life, its excessively authoritarian European rules were, she wrote to a friend, "dreadful walls to a burning soul wild as mine." Mother Seton prevailed in her struggle and continued to lead the Sisters of Charity until 1821, when she died of tuberculosis at the age of 47. She helped launch a tradition of Catholic community service that saw schools, hospitals, and orphanages emerge all across the continent, keeping pace with the great migrations of settlers into undeveloped territories. With her deep devotion to the Eucharist as well as to a vocation of service, she served as a role model for many Catholics in the decades following her death. In 1856 Mother Seton's nephew James Roosevelt Bayley—the first bishop of Newark—established Seton Hall College (later University), the first Catholic college in America operated under diocesan auspices (as opposed to a religious order). In 1975 Elizabeth Ann Bayley Seton was canonized as the first American-born saint of the church.

In the early years of the nation, the great majority of American Catholics, like most of their fellow citizens, were more concerned with pursuing opportunities for themselves and their families than with issues of church governance. Between the 1780s and the 1830s Catholics were as likely to be found in the rural South and along the western frontier as in the growing cities of the Northeast. An African-American Catholic fur trader, Jean-Baptiste Point du Sable, was the first settler of the community that became Chicago, and a Sulpician priest, Gabriel Richard, built Detroit's first schools and even held a seat in Congress as the delegate of the Michigan Territory.

Four new American dioceses were created in 1808—at New York, Boston, Philadelphia, and Bardstown, Kentucky, a thriving center of

Catholic frontier life just south of Louisville. The first Catholic church west of the Allegheny Mountains was erected at Holy Cross, Kentucky, in 1792, but many other Catholics in outlying communities soon longed for churches of their own, along with priests to administer the sacraments. Stephen T. Badin, a French missionary who was the first priest ordained in the United States, reported to Bishop John Carroll in 1796 that "probably there is not in all your diocese as large congregations as are those in Kentucky, and they are increasing from day to day; there is not a Catholic here that does not bitterly lament at finding himself deprived of those means of salvation that were to be had in Maryland."

The shortage of priests on the frontier made the work of the Catholic women's religious communities more crucial than ever before. Although prior to 1900 the church officially recognized only one option for women's religious life—communities of cloistered nuns who took "solemn" vows—several communities of religious sisters who pursued active vocations in teaching and service had emerged in Europe in the 17th century. The contemplative life, (a life devoted to prayer and solitude), however, remained the ideal, and women in conventional, noncloistered communities were often required to undergo the same rigorous spiritual practices as contemplative nuns. Three pioneer women in Kentucky—Mary Rhodes, Christina Stuart, and Nancy Havern—founded the Sisters of Loretto in 1812, under the guidance of an austere Belgian missionary, Father Charles Nerinckx. The Sisters of Loretto, the first American sisterhood without official ties to a European community, opened schools in Kentucky, Missouri, and other parts of the Midwest and Southwest. In 1813

Central Kentucky was the hub of frontier Catholicism in the early years of the 19th century. Nelson, Marion, and Washington counties were home to a growing number of Catholics who migrated from Maryland.

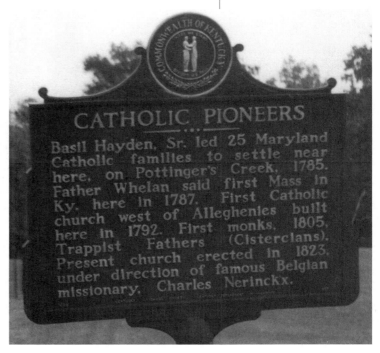

CATHOLIC PIONEERS

Basil Hayden, Sr. led 25 Maryland Catholic families to settle near here, on Pottinger's Creek, 1785. Father Whelan said first Mass in Ky. here in 1787. First Catholic church west of Alleghenies built here in 1792. First monks, 1805, Trappist Fathers (Cistercians). Present church erected in 1823, under direction of famous Belgian missionary, Charles Nerinckx.

Frontier Sisters

Rose Philippine Duchesne was a French missionary and a member of the Society of the Sacred Heart, a religious community for women. In this letter of February 15, 1819, to Madeleine Sophie Barat, the founder of the order, Mother Duchesne describes the joys and hardships of her community's work in Missouri. Rose Philippine Duchesne was canonized a saint by Pope John Paul II in 1988.

Very Reverend Mother:

A few days ago I received from New Orleans a letter dated May 4 and addressed to Father Martial, who is coming to St. Louis, and one from the Bishop written six months ago which describes so accurately what one may expect in this country that I thought it would be of interest to you. The second from Monsigneur was written quite lately and has to do with our going to Florissant. One must spend here a winter—even a mild one such as this—to realize that for the time being at least we can only vegetate in St. Charles, doing none of the good that is promised elsewhere. But it would cost me too much to abandon so many interesting children, many of whom will one day belong to the Sacred Heart, and I believe it essential to leave Sister Eugenie here for the present. With Sister Marguerite to assist her, she could easily manage our day school, especially if she had some young girls to help with the teaching. Many are spoken of, and while waiting for them to offer themselves we already have our one postulant [candidate for admission into the order], who is adapting herself to religious life and who can act as interpreter with English-speaking people. She still has six months to learn French, the study of which is developing her. Mother Eugenie is loved by her school; when at the close of her retreat she returned to them the children received her with such tears of joy that she herself wept. All cried, and since we have made known that we may be going to Florissant several of the older girls say: "I shall then pack up and go with you," and the younger ones ask to be taken along, saying that they are begging this of the Sacred Heart of Jesus. If we were only not so badly off we should be able to do very much good by taking some of the children with us, but what can we do without either lodging or provisions?

The Bishop was quite mistaken in thinking that we should be able to house here twenty-five pupils; there is not even room for sixteen, and, as it is, the beds have to be put up at night and removed in the morning. As the country beyond the Missouri River cannot furnish pupils able to pay, we can have only one day school. We see the poor children coming, famished and barefoot, to school along frozen roads and wearing only the lightest of dresses. You see, Reverend Mother, that, obliged as we are to give up our boarding school here, it would be dreadful to leave these poor children without giving them instruction. In four months many have learned to read and to write. They now know the whole little catechism, a number of hymns and prayers for Benediction and they are able to do all the singing. I hope that you will approve of two of us staying here, as such is the wish of his Lordship. Yesterday was a happy day. Father Porter, a young priest who came up with us from New Orleans, paid us a visit, asking us to make room for several more pupils. He is being sent to New Madrid, the seat of the earthquakes, which are felt almost as far as St. Charles; no priest has been to that village for twenty years. Another young priest, Father De La Croix, a Fleming, and our extraordinary confessor, has just come back from a part of Missouri which no missionaries had yet visited. There are now two stations there, one at Cote Sans Dessein, which he has consecrated to the Apostle, St. Paul, and where there are twenty-two families; the other, at Boonslick or Franklin, he has dedicated to St. Francis de Sales. There he gave a mission attended even by Protestants and fruitful for the Catholics. Some Protestants there are allowing their children to be instructed in the true faith by a catechist lately appointed.

another teaching order, the Sisters of Charity of Nazareth, was founded in a small community near Bardstown.

The members of women's religious communities working along the frontier pursued a shared vocation, as one sister explained, based "not so much in words as in deeds, that is, by a following of Christ's self-sacrificing love in the service and salvation of others." During the early and middle decades of the 19th century, a time when many American women were largely confined to the home, sisters brought their ministry to schools, orphanages, and hospitals across the United States, providing services that complemented those of, and occasionally substituted for, public agencies. When a cholera epidemic devastated New Orleans in 1837, sisters of the Ursuline order took financial responsibility for a state-owned orphanage. Following a similar outbreak in Baltimore, the city council dedicated a monument to two Sisters of Charity who had died after offering "services which were given without compensation."

Members of women's religious communities located in remote rural areas performed the same grueling manual labors as men. Although the conditions of life in these American communities were much more difficult than those found in their European counterparts, which were usually cloistered, the sisters were often required to combine a demanding spiritual regimen with exhausting physical work. Mother Rose Philippine Duchesne of the Society of the Sacred Heart, a French congregation, wrote from Missouri in 1821 that if the Jesuit missionaries working in Siberia "are looking for a mission field with the same type of work and the same climate during a good part of the year, they might come to our section of the globe." In 1824 Bishop Benedict Flaget of Bardstown informed a colleague that "in the space of eleven years, we have lost twenty-four religious [members of the community], and not one of them had yet reached the age of thirty years."

Many women's religious communities that were founded in Europe successfully adapted to their new environment and gradually assumed an American character. In 1836 a French community, the Sisters of St. Joseph, was invited to open a school for the deaf by Joseph Rosati, Bishop

of St. Louis. From their headquarters on a bluff overlooking the Mississippi river at Carondelet, Missouri, the Sisters of St. Joseph launched an
ambitious program of building schools, hospitals, and orphanages across
the nation. In addition to French-born sisters, the community attracted
immigrant women from Irish, German, and Canadian backgrounds as
well as a growing number of American-born women. In 1860 a new
"American" constitution was adopted by the order, effectively severing its
ties with French authorities. By then, however, the Sisters of St. Joseph's
programs were so widely dispersed that some of their establishments
came under the control of local bishops rather than the female superior
general in Carondelet. This arrangement exposed ongoing tensions
between sisters and male church authorities, but it also reflected the
desire of women's religious communities to respond creatively to local
needs. Sisters of St. Joseph taught American Indians in the Minnesota territory, African Americans in St. Louis, and members of European immigrant communities in urban parishes.

One French community that thrived while maintaining close ties to
the homeland—the Society of the Sacred Heart—was blessed by the able
leadership of Mother Duchesne, who led a group of missionaries to St.
Louis in 1818. In explaining to her French superior why the sisters did
not live behind the walls of a cloister as dictated by church law, Mother
Duchesne wrote, with only slight exaggeration, "There is not a wall with-
in a thousand miles of here." Mother Duchesne presided over the estab-
lishment of six schools before embarking on a mission to the Potawatomi
Indians at Sugar Creek, Kansas, in 1841. The Potawatomi dubbed her
Quah-Kah-Ka-num-ad, or "Woman Who Always Prays." Rose Philippine
Duchesne died in 1852 at the age of 83 and was canonized by Pope John
Paul II in 1988.

When Mother Duchesne arrived in St. Louis, that community was
still under the jurisdiction of the New Orleans diocese, whose bishop,
William DuBourg, had once served as spiritual director for Mother
Elizabeth Seton in Maryland. By the time he returned to France in 1826,
DuBourg had also served as president of Georgetown (founded in 1789),

Rose Philippine Duchesne
was born in Grenoble,
France, and came to the
United States in 1818 as a
member of the Society of
the Sacred Heart. She was
known for her deep piety
and a willingness to per-
form arduous manual
labor at her community's
frontier outposts.

St. Louis University moved to its current location in 1888. DuBourg Hall (foreground) is the main administration building. Behind it is St. Francis Xavier Church, also known as the College Church.

the nation's first Catholic college, and had helped launch the academy that became Saint Louis University, the first U.S. college founded west of the Mississippi River. DuBourg's busy career reflected the prevalence of European-born leadership within American Catholicism and also showed how dependent the church was on a small core group of missionaries at a time when the nation was expanding its boundaries at a dizzying pace.

Whereas DuBourg personified a French Catholicism that remained wary of American culture, Bishop John England of Charleston, South Carolina, brought traditions of Irish Catholicism to his leadership of an extensive diocese that encompassed North and South Carolina as well as Georgia. A native of the southern Irish coastal city of Cork, England became involved as a young priest in the struggle for Catholic emancipation from British laws that denied the Irish their religious and political rights.

John England's first two requests to be sent to America were turned down, but in 1820, at the age of 33, he was appointed Charleston's first bishop. He quickly discovered that the legal and social status of the tiny population of Catholics in America was very different from that in Ireland, where a persecuted majority was ruled by a foreign power. England informed a Savannah, Georgia resident in 1829 that, on his initial tour of the diocese, he "found one small brick church in North Carolina, two frame churches and one log church in Georgia, being a total of four. The number of communicants was in South Carolina about 200, in Georgia 150, and in North Carolina 25, being in all about 375. The number of priests in South Carolina two, in Georgia one, in all three."

Despite these differences, however, Bishop England concluded that the same ideals utilized by Catholics in Ireland to gain religious freedom could be applied to the American situation as well. England was a staunch advocate of the separation of church and state who believed that the truths of his faith would become evident to citizens of a free society. "There never was a union of church and state which did not bring serious evils to religion," he wrote in the *United States Catholic Miscellany,* the newspaper he founded in 1822. "I am convinced that a total separation from the temporal government is the most natural and safest for the church."

As a Catholic bishop, John England desired the greatest freedom for the church to pursue its mission free of interference from the state, but he also opposed expanded powers for lay trustees, including a group that had exercised considerable control over the affairs of St. Mary's Church in

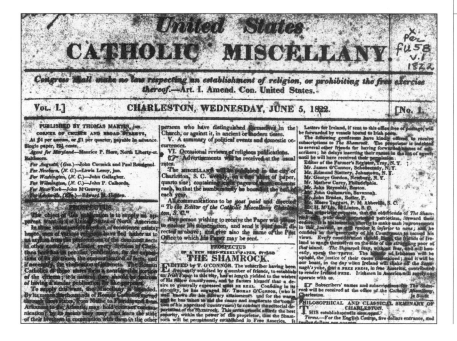

The first issue of the *United States Catholic Misellany* was published on June 5, 1822. The masthead bears a quotation from the First Amendment to the U.S. Constitution: "Congress shall make no law respecting an establishment of religion, or prohibiting the free exercise thereof."

Charleston. England refused to accept the designation of St. Mary's as the diocesan cathedral, choosing instead to build his own. In 1823 he wrote a *Constitution for the Diocese of Charleston* in order to provide a model of the proper balance, as he saw it, between the desires of the laity for influence in the church and the obligations of priests and bishops to provide leadership and enforce church authority. England's *Constitution* provided for an elected vestry (a governing body with responsibility for day to day operations as opposed to spiritual matters) in each parish with the power to appoint lay workers in the church. Parishes were also expected to choose members of a House of Lay Delegates who would meet with the House of Clergy at annual diocesan conventions. These conventions were authorized to present advice and requests to the bishop, but only the House of Clergy held authority over the spiritual matters of the diocese's religious institutions.

John England viewed the Roman Catholic Church as "an undying, perpetual and still living body." His belief that the relationship between believers and their church constituted a "voluntary covenant" struck a deep chord in American religious tradition, but England was ultimately unsuccessful in convincing many wary Protestants that Catholics readily embraced America's republican system of civil government. At the same time, he had to contend with two conflicting groups of Catholics: trustees who wanted more power for elite members of the laity, and traditionalists who feared that England's innovations were introducing too many democratic procedures into a church that was deeply hierarchical in its organization. Because England's fellow bishops tended to share the latter view, his ideas were resisted in other dioceses.

England's goal in establishing the *United States Catholic Miscellany*, a contemporary observer noted, was that of "uniting scattered Catholics in the States . . . educating and encouraging them in the midst of dangers to the faith." One of England's sisters, Joanna Monica England, was the managing editor of the newspaper, the first Catholic paper in the United States, until her premature death in 1827. Joanna England made a significant financial contribution to the fledgling diocese of Charleston from her personal fortune, but her greatest gift to the diocese was the wise counsel she offered to her brother, who could be abrasive in his writings. When Joanna died at the age of 27, John England extolled her as "a sensible companion, a great literary aid. . . . She did more by the sacrifice of her money and of her comforts to establish the Diocese than was done by any other means I know."

Bishop England's voluminous writings dominated the editorial content of the *United States Catholic Miscellany.* Much of his work entailed defending the church from its many critics. In a well-known "Series of Letters to the Roman Catholics of the United States" in 1826, England wrote that, as an immigrant,

> I found what I was altogether unprepared for; that, in many of our States, a Roman Catholic, though legally and politically upon a level with his fellow citizens, was however to be looked upon, by reason of his religion, as in some degree morally degraded. I found that it was by no means considered a want of liberality, on the part of Protestants, to vilify the Catholic religion, and to use the harshest and most offensive terms when designating its practices; but that if a Catholic used any phrase however modified, which even insinuated any thing derogatory to the Protestant religion, he was marked out as a shocking bigot.

When Bishop England wrote this letter in 1826 there were approximately 250,000 Roman Catholics in the United States out of a total population of more than 11 million. They might indeed have encountered prejudice, as the bishop suggested, but the Catholic community was then too small and shared too much in common with the dominant Protestant majority to become a focal point of great national concern. Over the next three decades, however, the Catholic population would skyrocket to total more than 3 million, with the increase due largely to massive immigration from Europe. And as if this numerical increase was not startling enough in itself, these new Americans were "different": most were impoverished, and many spoke an unfamiliar language. They also practiced their religion in a fashion different from American Catholics and Protestants alike. The interaction of these immigrants with the customs of their new home would change America forever and usher in the century of the "immigrant church."

494

Chapter 3

The Rise of the Immigrant Church

"Coming on the harvest time of the year 1845, the crops looked splendid," recalled an Irish American of a fateful moment in world history, "but one fine morning in July there was a cry around that some blight had struck the potato stalks." Soon the "air was laded with a sickly odor of decay, as if the hand of death had stricken the potato field, and . . . everything growing in it was rotten."

From 1845 until the early 1850s, every potato harvest in Ireland was afflicted by a previously unknown fungus that destroyed the only source of food for most of that country's inhabitants. At least 1 million Irish people died of starvation, and another 1.8 million sought relief in North America. These famine migrants signaled the changing nature of America's population in that they made up the first wave of European refugees fleeing hunger and oppression who entered the United States between the 1840s and the early 1920s. Because the majority of these immigrants, who numbered in the millions, were Roman Catholics, they dramatically changed the course of America's religious history as well.

A small number of Irish settlers had been among the earliest inhabitants of the middle colonies in the mid 17th century, but until 1815 the Irish Americans remained a widely scattered and largely Protestant population, with roots in the Scottish communities transplanted to Northern Ireland by the British in the early 18th century. Between 1815 and 1845

Irish immigrants work in a drainage ditch beneath the tracks of the Boston and Albany Railroad near West Newton, Massachusetts. Throughout the 19th century, Irish Americans played a leading role in building the nation's transportation systems.

51

nearly 1 million Irish emigrants, Protestants and Catholics alike, made their way to the United States, seeking economic opportunity in the industrializing cities of the eastern seaboard. After 1845, however, the overwhelming majority of Irish immigrants were Catholic peasants fleeing poverty and famine. Irish peasant families were wholly dependent on the potato crop for their nourishment; they exported other crops to pay the increasing rents demanded by their absentee British and Irish landlords. When the blight wiped out virtually the entire Irish potato harvest in 1846, the English government responded with half-hearted relief measures, but by then virtually nothing could have prevented further catastrophe. Some were not sorry to see the Irish suffer. "In a few more years," wrote an editorialist in the *London Times* in 1848, "a Celtic Irishman will be as rare in Connemara as is the Red Indian on the shores of Manhattan."

The Irish embarked for North America on leaky vessels that became known as coffin ships. During an 1853 cholera epidemic, more than 10 percent of all Irish migrants died before they could see their new homeland. These perilous sea voyages set the tone for what was to come for all but the most fortunate of the Irish immigrants. While a few attained unimagined riches, the great majority endured grinding poverty and often dangerous employment, helping to build railroads, bridges, and canals.

In cities from Boston to Butte, Montana to San Francisco, Irish Catholics became the chief suppliers of unskilled labor for the rapidly expanding national economy. The typical Irish immigrant, wrote one laborer, "toils on, year after year, under a burning sun in summer, and an intense cold winter, to earn a miserable subsistence, and is not so happy in his position as he would be in his own country with a single acre to raise potatoes for himself and his family." All of the able-bodied members of Irish immigrant families were expected to find work, including unmarried daughters, who often toiled as domestic servants. In some cities more than three-quarters of the working Irish women were employed as domestics: cooking, cleaning, and helping raise the children of middle- and upper-income families while struggling in many cases to help support their own families.

The ordeal of the Irish was aggravated by the ethnic and religious prejudice they routinely encountered in the United States. Although such genteel Catholics as the Carroll family of Baltimore and the Carolinas had enjoyed widespread acceptance by Protestant Americans, the "poor Irish," an immigrant lamented in 1822, were often viewed "as belonging to a race of savages." A typical advertisement in a New York City newspaper in the 1840s read, "Woman Wanted—to do general housework . . . English, Scotch, Welsh, German or any country or color except Irish." Self-appointed defenders of America's Protestant heritage, often called nativists, sometimes expressed their indignation by torching Catholic churches, the most conspicuous symbol of the Irish presence in America's largest cities.

In 1832 a young woman named Rebecca Reed began telling tales of her alleged "escape" from a convent school run by Ursuline nuns in Charlestown, Massachusetts, though she had actually been expelled from the school for dishonesty. Her claim that girls were held there against their will by the nuns inflamed the hostility of numerous townsfolk. On August 10, 1834, a leading Congregationalist minister, Lyman Beecher, preached a sermon in Charlestown on "The Devil and the Pope of Rome," a theme that was addressed by other ministers in town that same day. The following night, rioters gathered at the gates of the convent. When the Ursuline headmistress warned them to disperse, claiming that the bishop "has twenty thousand Irishmen at his command in Boston and they will whip you all into the sea," the mob invaded the convent grounds. Drunken rioters donned nuns' clothing while others set rooms afire. The homes of several Irish Americans in Charlestown were also burned down. A jury later acquitted all but one of the alleged arsonists.

Rebecca Reed's tale was published by a group of nativists in 1835 under the title *Six Months in a Convent;* it sold 10,000 copies during its first week in print and more than 200,000 in all. Such popular literary accounts of the alleged depravity found in convents helped fuel grassroots anti-Catholicism in the period. The best-known example of this literary form, Maria Monk's *Awful Disclosures of the Hotel Dieu Nunnery in*

Sensational accounts of imaginary events in Catholic convents helped fan the flames of bigotry. These 1836 illustrations depict, from top, "A Nun Stabbing a Priest," "Death-Pit—Trap-Door—Cell," and "The Smothering of the Nun."

Montreal (1836) sold 300,000 copies, an enormous figure at a time when the nation's population was less than 20 million. It was the best-selling work of literature in America prior to the publication in 1852 of *Uncle Tom's Cabin* (whose author, Harriet Beecher Stowe, was the daughter of the Reverend Lyman Beecher). Monk's fabricated tale of illicit relations between priests and nuns at a Montreal convent appealed not only to rabid anti-Catholics but to many Americans who believed that such secretive organizations as the Masons and the Mormon church did not properly belong in an open and democratic society. Catholicism was viewed by many as both foreign and mysterious, themes that provoked highly mixed feelings in mid-19th-century America.

The mobs who attacked convents and read anti-Catholic literature were motivated at least in part by curiosity, because the life of Catholic women's religious communities was so alien to their experience. At the Ursuline convent in Charlestown most of the students were not even Catholic but were the daughters of prominent local Unitarians. The members of this liberal Protestant denomination were often at odds with the more conservative Congregationalists (inheritors of the New England Puritan tradition) who dominated the community. Many of these girls were themselves familiar with the literature of popular anti-Catholicism, but their very presence at the convent school indicated that the nuns were admired for the educational component of their vocation if not their cloistered lifestyle.

With the arrival of masses of impoverished Irish immigrants in the 1840s, however, the attitudes of many Americans toward Catholics hardened into bitter hostility. Rioting, church burnings, and armed skirmishes between Catholics and nativists broke out in Philadelphia, St. Louis, Louisville, and Detroit during the decade, with significant loss of life on all sides. Many Irish Americans who had emigrated by choice in the years prior to the famine now grew disillusioned with their new nation and came to view themselves as exiles from their ancestral homeland. The famine emigrants were in no position to return to Ireland, however. Their poverty, which often led to alcoholism and sometimes to insanity and criminality, convinced some Americans that Irish Catholics were inherently depraved. Others sought ways to help the rural Irish adjust to urban America, but in the absence of state or federal agencies dedicated to the

Shortly after nativist rioting broke out near Philadelphia in 1844, James W. Porter wrote "See Our Torn Flag Still Waving." The sheet music for the song was illustrated by a tattered American flag, which became a symbol for anti-Catholics who claimed that Irish immigrants had mutilated a flag during the Philadelphia upheavals.

plight of newly arrived immigrants the Catholic Church, and more precisely the local parish church, quickly became the most important resource for the physical as well as spiritual welfare of the famine Irish.

In the 1840s and 1850s immigrant Catholics may have been unpopular, but an increasingly organized church ensured that they were not entirely powerless. John Hughes, the Irish-born bishop of New York, was the most flamboyant of a new generation of leaders for an immigrant church bearing little resemblance to the church of Bishop John Carroll. Hughes, who was once called by a priest of his diocese "a tyrant, but with feeling," did not shrink from religious controversy with Protestants but militantly defended his flock of 200,000 Catholics (in a diocese that originally encompassed all of New York State and part of New Jersey) against insults both real and imagined. In 1840 Hughes confronted New York's Public School Society, an organization of leading Protestants who dictated the curriculum of the city's schools. A textbook entitled *The Irish Heart* offered a view of Irish Catholics prevalent at the time in its description of a fictional character receiving the sacrament of Penance (through which sinners are reconciled both to God and the church by confessing their sins to a priest): "When Phelim had laid up a good stock of sins he now and then . . . got relaaf by confissing them out o' the way . . . and sealed up his soul with a wafer, and returned quite invigorated for the perpetration of new offenses."

Bishop Hughes fought for a public school system that would respect the diversity of its students. He wanted religious instruction entrusted to appropriate figures from the various churches represented in the school population. Catholics in New York were extremely loyal to the Democratic party—which had reached out to immigrants as a potent base of support—but when some Democratic legislators failed to back the bishop's school proposals, Hughes decided in 1841 to run his own independent slate of candidates in local elections. When his candidates (along with those Democrats who supported him) swept to victory, New York legislators, having awakened to the magnitude of Catholic political power, quickly moved to take control of the schools out of the hands of the Public School Society. Although Bishop Hughes now declared the public schools safe for Catholic children, he had already decided to launch a massive, costly system of separate Catholic schools.

Bishop John Hughes's militant defense of his immigrant flock signaled a new era in Catholic America Hughes was appointed archbishop in 1850, which meant that he exercised supervisory jurisdiction over several new dioceses created in the region. In laying the cornerstone of New York City's massive St. Patrick's Cathedral in 1858 he triumphantly proclaimed, before a crowd of more than 100,000, that "the spiritual descendants of St. Patrick have been outcasts from their native land and have been scattered over the earth. . . . The churches which they have erected . . . are the most fitting headstones to commemorate . . . the honorable history of the Irish people." He also told the Irish

St. Patrick's Cathedral in 1894. When construction of the massive church began in 1858, critics scorned its location far north of central Manhattan. The beloved cathedral's location in the heart of midtown today makes it one of America's most popular tourist attractions.

Catholics in the throng that they could "laugh to scorn" those who ridiculed their customs and religion. Hughes's blunt, confrontational remarks aroused the ire of the *New York Times,* which chided the bishop for his "bad taste which, of late years, has more or less characterized everything His Grace has said or written outside the immediate sphere of his archepiscopal duties."

John Hughes and many other bishops in the mid 19th century recognized that impoverished Irish immigrants were comfortable only with priests from their homeland. In 1870 an Irish missionary priest traveling in western Pennsylvania described his reception by an immigrant community: "In a short time the word was spread that an Irish priest had arrived—all the villages forthwith came to see me & hear about the old country. How delighted they were & what an affection they have for every thing Irish." Because the great majority of Irish immigrants were English-speaking (the Irish language had been outlawed by the British and was still spoken only in scattered pockets of Ireland), the multitude of new parish churches established for Irish Americans were soon considered by priests and parishioners alike as unmistakably American churches.

Catholic immigrants from countries other than Ireland would often view their own churches in a different light. Approximately 1.7 million German Catholics migrated to the United States between 1820 and 1920. Between 1820 and the 1880s, Germans made up by far the second-largest Catholic immigrant group in America. Even though the Germans, unlike the Irish, spoke a "foreign" language, German Catholic immigrants possessed certain key advantages over Catholics hailing from the Emerald Isle. They tended to come from more prosperous backgrounds and often boasted vocational skills that were highly desired in an industrializing America where they might find work as carpenters, bakers, brewers, or tailors. The German Catholic immigrant communities were most heavily concentrated in a region within a triangle from Cincinnati to Milwaukee to St. Louis and back, cities that were not as well established as their counterparts in the East and were therefore somewhat less susceptible to outbreaks of nativism. German Catholics were also more successful in building harmonious relationships with Protestants from their homeland than were Irish-American Catholics.

The great majority of German Catholics, however, settled not in cities but in farming communities. Many of these immigrants came from small landholding families and they were highly attracted to the fertile, inexpensive farmland available in the Midwest. These communities were invariably centered around a newly created parish, with churches staffed by priests who traveled from Germany to minister to their compatriots. The number of German priests in the United States increased from 50 in 1843 (to serve a German-American population of 300,000) to 1,169 in 1869 (when the total number of German-American Catholics had surely surpassed one million, though precise figures are impossible to determine). By that year slightly more than one-third of American priests were German speakers, nearly all of whom were German born.

German Americans were quite clear in their desire to maintain the customs and language of their native land. Their determination to establish "national" parishes eventually produced a conflict with the Irish-dominated leadership of the Catholic Church in America. Parishes normally include all the Catholics residing within the given territorial boundaries, whatever their origins. Unlike territorial parishes, however, national parishes were designed to minister to the members of a particular ethnic group. Although the desire for national parishes struck some Catholics as divisive, German Americans, like the members of many subsequent immigrant groups, found that expressions of pride in one's heritage actually contributed to the process of becoming American. The new ethnic identities that immigrants created for themselves in their new country blended loyalty to ancient traditions with appreciation for the opportunities U.S. citizenship promised.

Ethnicity is a flexible concept employed not merely to highlight a person's national origins but also to indicate the creative process through which individuals form a personal identity as members of a social group. Ever since the 1840s, the great majority of Catholics in the United States have sustained their ethnic as well as religious traditions while proudly claiming full-fledged membership in the American community.

French-speaking Alsatian immigrants in Castroville, Texas, formed a chapter of the St. Louis Society in the late 19th century. Alsace was a region located between France and Germany, claimed by each of the two countries at different points in history.

Henriette Delille, a free woman of color from a prominent New Orleans family, was an early feminist, educator, social worker, and co-founder of one of the first orders of African-American Catholic nuns, the Sisters of the Holy Family. She began at age 14 as a lay catechist, teaching slaves on plantations about Christianity.

One ethnic group that enjoyed far less freedom to define itself than others was the small community of African-American Catholics found in pre–Civil War America. In Maryland, the slaves of Catholic planters were often baptized into the church. The migration of Maryland slave owners to Kentucky at the beginning of the 19th century resulted in the creation of a significant African-American community in the Nelson County area. Slaves were also regularly baptized in Mobile, Alabama, and in New Orleans, where a Catholic community of "free people of color"—the offspring of white men and African-American women—gained prominence in the early 19th century.

In 1836 Henriette Delille, a free woman of color whose great-great grandmother was owned by the royal engineer of the king of France, helped to establish the Sisters of the Presentation in New Orleans, a group made up of white and Creole (mixed race) women. The community soon disbanded, however, under pressure from local Catholic authorities and the civil government, which both objected to the group's interracial character. In 1842 a French-born priest, the Abbé Rousselon, persuaded the local bishop to permit Delille and Juliette Gaudin—a Cuban-born woman of mixed racial ancestry—to form a new group, the Sisters of the Holy Family. Five years later a lay Association of the Holy Family was formed to aid the sisters in their work, which included schools operated for the children of free blacks as well as a ministry to the sick and the aged. The Sisters of the Holy Family carried out their work despite continued hostility from segments of the local community. The sisters were not permitted to make their public vows until 1852 and could not wear their religious attire, or habits, in public until 1872, a decade after the death of Henriette Delille.

Haitian refugees of color also contributed to the formation of an African-American Catholic community. In 1831 Elizabeth Lange, a Cuban-born woman of Haitian parentage, organized—with assistance from James Hector Joubert, a white Sulpician priest—the first African-American women's religious community in America, the Oblate Sisters of

Providence. Over the objections of many white Catholics, the sisters opened schools for black children near Baltimore, the order's headquarters. When Baltimore was hit by a devastating outbreak of cholera in 1832, the entire community offered to volunteer as nurses. As Father Joubert recalled, "They all cried that they were ready to undertake it, that they should find much happiness in being able to serve our Lord in the person of the sick."

Another American Catholic of Haitian ancestry, Pierre Toussaint, a former slave, became one of the most prominent and beloved Catholics in New York City in the first half of the 19th century. A highly successful hairdresser, he was once described by a New York socialite as "the fashionable coiffeur of the day." Toussaint and his wife, Juliette, were major benefactors of the Catholic Orphan Asylum and opened their own home to impoverished black children, providing shelter and education until the children were prepared to take care of themselves.

Despite the efforts of these prominent individuals and communities, however, American Catholicism's treatment of African Americans did not differ notably from that of other Christian denominations in the decades prior to the Civil War. Until the 1830s, Jesuits in Maryland owned slaves, though many younger members of the community wished to see them freed. The slaves were sold rather than freed in 1837–38, partly in order to raise capital for educational enterprises. Other religious orders with properties in southern states owned slaves as well. In 1839 Pope Gregory XVI condemned the slave trade rather than the institution of slavery itself. Like members of other Christian denominations, Catholics differed among themselves over the issue of slavery throughout the first half of the 19th century, with geography playing a large role in determining opinion. Cincinnati's archbishop John Purcell strongly believed in the abolition of slavery, but in Louisville, across the Ohio River 100 miles to the southwest of Cincinnati, the *Catholic Advocate* advertised the sale of slaves, sometimes accompanied by such notes as "I would prefer selling them to a Catholic." In 1842, Bishop

The son of a slave woman from Haiti, Pierre Toussaint became a prominent businessman in New York and a leader of the African-American Catholic community. For more than 60 years he attended a daily 6 A.M. mass at St. Peter's Church in lower Manhattan.

John England of Charleston, South Carolina, tried to argue in the *United States Catholic Miscellany* that in 1839 the pope had opposed the slave trade but not slave ownership, an issue that England insisted had to be addressed by the individual state legislatures.

Some northern Catholics were more opposed to abolitionists than to slavery. Patrick Donahoe, editor of the *Boston Pilot,* promoted a widely shared view that abolitionism was a strictly Protestant crusade with anti-Catholic overtones. Many abolitionists were indeed hostile to Irish-American Catholics. Southern apologists for slavery often claimed the Irish workers in the North were treated worse than slaves, an argument that embarrassed abolitionists, many of whom believed the Irish had no one to blame but themselves for their poverty. The famed Massachusetts abolitionist William Lloyd Garrison described Irish Catholics as a "mighty obstacle in the way of negro emancipation." Michael Walsh, an Irish Protestant immigrant who represented a heavily Catholic New York City district in the U.S. House of Representatives, exclaimed from the floor of the House in 1854 that "the only difference between the negro slave of the South and the white wage slave of the North is that the one has a master without asking for him, and the other has to beg for the privilege of becoming a slave."

In the early 1850s the American Party emerged as a potent, if short-lived, expression of political anti-Catholicism. Popularly known as the Know-Nothings (because members of a related nativist organization customarily replied "I know nothing" when asked about their activities), the American Party exploited anxieties over immigrants and Catholics. In the late 1850s, however, when the new Republican party merged nativists and abolitionists into a powerful antislavery vehicle willing to confront the South head-on, Northern immigrant laborers generated less controversy than in the past.

Southern Catholics, while relatively few in number, generally supported the Confederacy once the Civil War began in 1861, though unlike some Protestant denominations there was no formal split between northern and southern Catholics. Certain members of elite southern Catholic communities, such as that found in Louisiana, played important roles in

the Confederate cause. General Pierre G. T. Beauregard was a leading military strategist for the Confederate army, and two cousins, Louis and Paul Hebert, West Point graduates and brilliant engineers, were both deeply devout Catholics and leaders of the Confederacy in Louisiana. A notorious Confederate spy, Belle Boyd (the "Rebel Rose") was a Maryland Catholic, while a descendant of the Carroll family of Maryland served as a member of the Arkansas delegation to the Confederate Congress. Father Abram Ryan, a noncommissioned chaplain to troops from Georgia, wrote ardent verse on behalf of the South and became known as the unofficial poet laureate of the Confederacy.

A green-and-gold-clad Irish-Catholic brigade of the first Virginia Infantry received the blessing of Bishop John McGill in the basement of Richmond's St. Peter's Cathedral; then, at the Battle of Bull Run, they fought the legendary Fighting 69th, an Irish-American regiment from New York. The 69th also fought gallantly and took heavy losses at the

In the 1944 Philadelphia riot, "Know-Nothings" wearing tall beaver hats burned two famous old Catholic churches, fought off the state militia, and killed 24 people.

63

ATLANTA CAMPAIGN.
ARMY OF THE CUMBERLAND.

EASTER SUNDAY 1864.
1861. 1865.

HOLY COMMUNION.

SISTERS IN FIELD HOSPITAL.

The Rev. P. P. Cooney celebrates Easter Sunday Mass in 1864 for members of the 35th Indiana Volunteers serving in the Union Army's Atlanta campaign. Father Cooney was a member of the Congregation of the Holy Cross (C.S.C.), the French religious order that founded the University of Notre Dame in 1842.

Battle of Gettysburg over July 3–4, 1863. Just one week later, bloody Draft Riots broke out in New York City, where Irish Americans were being conscripted into the Union Army in greater proportion than members of other ethnic groups. Many Irish were also resentful of local African Americans who had served as "scab" (replacement) labor during a recent strike of Irish longshoremen. Rioters burned an orphanage for black children and assaulted African Americans in the streets during four days and nights of lawlessness. The offices of the *New York Tribune,* a nativist paper, were also destroyed by rioters. In the mayhem, 105 people were killed, including 11 African Americans and 10 members of the police and militia attempting to quell the riot.

Irish Americans and African Americans often lived side by side in the poorest neighborhoods of American cities, where they shared much in common. (After visiting Ireland during the famine, the African-American leader Frederick Douglass noted the similar depth of feeling expressed in Irish and slave songs. He was "much affected," he wrote at the time, by the "wailing notes" of Irish songs that reminded him of the "wild notes" of slave songs.) The Draft Riots marked a low point in the history of Catholic immigration to the United States, although *Harper's* magazine, a publication not known for its sympathy toward the Irish, lauded the efforts of Archbishop John Hughes to restore order in the city (which proved to be the final public appearance for the aged Hughes). The *Harper's* editorialist noted further that "Irishmen helped to rescue the colored orphans in the asylum from the hands of the rioters; that a large proportion of the police, who behaved throughout the riot with the most exemplary gallantry, are Irishmen; that the Roman Catholic priesthood to a man used their influence on the side of the law."

The Draft Riots were hardly representative of the efforts of northern Catholics on behalf of the Union cause. Some 150,000 Irish and 175,000 German Catholic Americans fought for the Union during the Civil War. Major General Philip Sheridan, a son of Irish immigrants, became a renowned leader of the Union army who made a special point of praising the valor of Catholic troops who fought under his command. The Irish Brigade organized by Thomas Meagher absorbed terrible losses at the battles of Fredericksburg and Chancellorsville in Virginia. Nearly 800,000 Catholic immigrants worked in war plants or on farms vacated by men who had joined the Union army.

More than 600 sisters from twenty-one religious communities served as nurses during

A recruitment poster seeks Irish-American volunteers for the Fifth Regiment of the famed "Corcoran Legion," Union Army. Thirty-eight Union regiments bore the word "Irish" in their names.

65

the Civil War. Sisters made up twenty percent of the nursing corps on the battlefields and in the hospitals of both the Union and the Confederacy. The service performed by these women helped to lessen anti-Catholicism: for several decades after the war many non-Catholics used the terms "sisters of charity" or "sisters of mercy" as a generic term for all members of women's religious communities.

The many sacrifices made by Catholics during the Civil War won a measure of respect for the church and its people. Yet after the war *Harper's* continued to publish anti-Catholic cartoons by the celebrated illustrator Thomas Nast, who satirized the growing Irish-American influence in Tammany Hall, New York's powerful Democratic party organization. The editors now explained that Nast was opposed not to the church but to its alleged involvement with the political process, a theme that would persist over the next century.

Because the great majority of American Catholics lived in the north, the Union's triumph enhanced the confidence of the immigrant church as well. Devotionalism, a distinctive brand of spirituality highly attractive to Irish and German-Catholic Americans, flourished in the post–Civil War era. Devotional Catholicism is a term that covers a wide range of spiritual practices, from the recitation of the rosary (from the Latin for "rose garden," the rosary consists of sets of recited prayers, including the Hail Mary and the Lord's Prayer; stringed rosary beads are often used to keep count of the prayers) to special prayers to Mary, the mother of Jesus, or to patron saints of various causes. Devotionalism is often considered a popular, spontaneous form of Catholic worship, because the devotions are performed outside the setting of the sacred liturgy and therefore do not necessarily require the presence of a priest. In mid-19th-century America, however, devotional practices were often promoted by members of religious orders or itinerant preachers intent on organizing a widely scattered religious community. In this way devotionalism represented not just a set of ritual practices but a strategy for unifying an immigrant church across lines of region, ethnicity, and class.

Devotional Catholicism became a central feature of parish missions, a Catholic version of the revival meetings that had long been a fixture in

many Protestant denominations. Every four or five years a guest preacher, who was often a priest of the Jesuit, Redemptorist, or Paulist orders, was invited to a parish to lead a mission. Redemptorist priests were members of the Congregation of the Most Holy Redeemer, a religious order founded in Italy that established its first U.S. mission in 1832. The Missionary Society of St. Paul, or Paulist order, was founded in 1858 by five former Redemptorists, all of whom were native-born American converts to Catholicism. The Paulist order was the first priestly community founded in the United States. While the Redemptorists initially focused their efforts on the German-American immigrant communities, the Paulists sought to introduce Catholicism to native-born audiences.

Parish missions varied somewhat, depending on the background of the preacher, but they shared certain features in common. A leaflet distributed in 1873 in a New York City parish described that mission as "a time

An 1871 cartoon for *Harper's Weekly* by Thomas Nast depicts Catholic bishops' mitres (headgear), shaped like crocodile heads, invading American shores. Virtuous Protestant women are dragged to the gallows by Irishmen, while New York's Democratic party headquarters (Tammany Hall) is drawn to resemble the Vatican's St. Peter's Basilica.

when God calls with a more earnest voice than at other times all persons, but sinners especially, to work out their salvation with fear and trembling . . . It is a time when you are exhorted, by the cross and blood of Christ, if indeed you have a spark of gratitude or love towards God, to turn your face to him with contrition." And in the same period, a Redemptorist priest remarked on the popular appeal of missions: "The church is frequently filled two hours before the time of the service. The porch, the steps, the windows even are crowded and hundreds go away disappointed . . . I have seen at least four thousand persons congregated in the streets adjacent to the New York Cathedral, besides the crowd inside."

Mission preachers insisted that their campaigns differed from Protestant revivals because they were grounded in the sacraments, rather than in preaching that appealed strictly to the emotions. The sacrament of Penance (confession) was the foundation of the parish mission, explained Father Walter Elliot, because "a patient searching of the heart done with calm deliberation" in the presence of a priest was essential before a genuine conversion could be achieved. The number of confessions skyrocketed during missions, as the ministers convinced devout and lukewarm Catholics alike of the centrality of the sacraments to their faith. While religious enthusiasm generally tapered off in the months following the close of a mission, this form of Catholic revivalism deeply influenced popular piety well into the 20th century.

The popularity of parish missions led directly to a great increase in the membership of Catholic confraternities, societies organized around a particular devotional practice. The special devotions of confraternities included veneration of the Sacred Heart of Jesus, devotions to the Blessed Virgin Mary, the praying of the rosary, and the wearing of scapulars, two small pieces of cloth tied together and draped over the shoulders. Scapulars had traditionally been worn by monks as a sign of devotion to Mary, so the smaller versions worn by lay people enabled them to cultivate a closer relationship to her as well.

Popular devotions inspired what are known as intercessory prayer, which are offered in the form of petitions on behalf of other persons and are directed to Jesus, Mary, or one of the saints. Intercessory prayers could also benefit the person who offered them: as a popular prayer book, *The Ursuline Manual* of 1857, explained, one might pray "to obtain the grace to conquer some fault" and to "acquire some virtue" as well as "for the conversion of some sinner; for those who are in the agonies of death; or for the suffering of the souls in purgatory." This devotional style was largely absent from U.S. Catholicism prior to the massive immigration of Irish and Germans in the 1840s and 1850s. Where the popular piety of Anglo-American Protestants and Catholics in that earlier era shared much in common, the rise of devotionalism signaled a major shift in the dominant religious style of American Catholics. In 1831 the French aristocrat Alexis de Tocqueville discovered while visiting the United States that "there are no Roman Catholic priests who show less taste for the minute individual observances, for the extraordinary or peculiar means of salvation . . . than the Roman Catholic priests of the United States." Within only a matter of decades, "minute individual observances" had become the foundation of American Catholic piety: the devotional style would prevail for the next one hundred years.

The greatly elevated stature of the Blessed Virgin Mary among Catholics in the middle of the 19th century was at the heart of devotionalism. As the mother of Jesus, Mary had always occupied an exalted place among Catholics, but her special role as mediatrix (mediator) between unworthy sinners and God began to slowly emerge in Europe around the 8th century. Eight hundred years later, Protestant reformers criticized Mary's status as recipient of special prayers, such as the Hail Mary. The Blessed Virgin's centrality in Catholic devotions grew even stronger with a series of apparitions (appearances) in the 19th century. Mary was reported to have appeared to a nun in Paris in 1830 and to children at the French town of La Salette in 1846. Apparitions were also reported elsewhere in Europe, but the most celebrated Marian visions occurred in the spring of 1858 near the town of Lourdes, in the Pyrenees mountains of southern France. A young peasant girl, Bernadette Soubirous, reported that she had seen and spoken with a woman in white on several occasions. After repeated queries from Bernadette, the woman finally declared: "I am the Immaculate Conception" (in 1854 the Church had made official the traditional Catholic view that Mary was conceived without sin and was therefore "free from all stain of original sin"). Though the visions suddenly ceased, people flocked to the site of the visions at Lourdes, especially those seeking miraculous cures from spring waters that Mary had instructed Bernadette to drink.

Marian devotions in the United States were intensified by the work of European missionaries. In 1842 Edward Sorin, a French missionary priest, founded a school in northern Indiana that eventually became the University of Notre Dame ("Our Lady"), a leading educational institution as well as a center of Marian activities. In 1844 Holy Cross sisters founded St. Mary's College for young women on land adjoining the Notre Dame campus. Father Sorin launched the journal *Ave Maria* (Hail Mary) in 1865; it quickly became one of the most popular Catholic publications in America. In 1877 a replica shrine of the grotto at Lourdes—where Bernadette first saw the Blessed Virgin Mary—was constructed on the Notre Dame campus. Father Sorin also played a role in the importation of bottled water from the spring at Lourdes, which was a highly desired commodity among American Catholics suffering from a wide variety of maladies. While Notre Dame was the epicenter of Marian devotions, Catholics across the nation prayed fervently for the Blessed Virgin Mary's protection and care.

In the middle and late years of the 19th century, the Blessed Virgin Mary appealed to some Protestant Americans, who viewed her as an exemplary mother and a symbol of purity. In general, however, Protestants viewed devotions to Mary with the same strongly mixed feelings they held toward Catholicism in general. Protestants, who generally favored simple, unadorned religious architecture and similarly forthright preaching, often found traditional Catholic ritual—along with the immigrants' style of devotional culture—to be overly ornate and even garish. Yet many Protestants also recognized that their own traditions were ultimately rooted in Catholicism. In the highly charged religious atmosphere of 19th-century America it was perhaps inevitable that many people who were born into Protestant families would find themselves exploring the Catholic tradition, and a significant number went on to become full-fledged converts, as Elizabeth Bayley Seton had done at the turn of the century.

One of the most controversial, yet revealing, conversions in the 19th century was that of Orestes Brownson, whose restless journey took him from the stern Congregationalism of his Vermont boyhood to unsatisfying stints as a Presbyterian, a Universalist (a Protestant denomination that taught that all souls would be saved), and a Unitarian, or believer in the moral teachings but not the divinity of Jesus Christ. Brownson was also a member of the Transcendentalist Club of Boston, where he befriended such luminaries as Ralph Waldo Emerson, Henry David Thoreau, and others who shared his quest for a new American spirituality free of any traces of the Calvinism of their New England Puritan ancestors, a tradition they now viewed as highly rigid and emotionally drab (named for the Swiss Protestant reformer John Calvin, Calvinism taught that human beings could not achieve salvation by their own efforts). In 1836 Brownson even tried starting a new religion, the Society for Christian Union and Progress.

In 1844, the same year he launched his celebrated journal *Brownson's Quarterly Review*, Orestes Brownson became a Catholic, which he remained until his death in 1876. In *The Convert*, an 1857 account of his long journey toward the church, Brownson conceded that right up until the moment of his conversion he had harbored negative views of Catholics and of church writings that "seemed to me ignorant of the ideas and wants of the non-Catholic world, engrossed with obsolete questions, and wanting in broad and comprehensive views." Brownson was a self-made Catholic convert who was attracted to the church by his own ideas of what it should offer to other Americans. Protestants objected that Catholics were not encouraged to think for themselves, due to doctrines such as papal infallibility [the view that the Holy Spirit guided the Church—through the bishops and pope—without error, a tradition that

"Politicians may do as they please, so long as they violate no rule of right, no principle of justice, no law of God; but in no world, in no order, or condition, have men the right to do wrong."
—Orestes Brownson

was altered with the proclamation in 1870 that the Pope himself acted infallibly]. Brownson responded in *The Convert* that a Catholic mind "is no more restricted in its freedom by the authoritative definitions of an infallible church than the cautious mariner by the charts and beacons that guide his course."

Along with many other Americans, Brownson was troubled by the social upheavals accompanying rapid industrialization. He felt that Catholicism offered a deeper, more orderly vision of the individual's relationship to society and to God than any of the other spiritual traditions he had sampled. Brownson could not, however, muster much sympathy for the throngs of Irish-Catholic immigrants whose religious practices did not resemble the rather idealized Roman Catholicism that had sparked his own conversion. Despite his great prominence as a Catholic writer and the honors bestowed upon him from Rome, Brownson remained isolated from the vibrant life of the immigrant church.

Isaac Hecker, a German American born in New York in 1819, was another notable convert who, like Brownson, spent some time in Transcendentalist circles before he too converted to Catholicism in 1844. The following year he wrote to Brownson: "The Church is all . . . I want her to crush me, so that she may be all in me, which she now is not. There is no use of compromise. There can be no looking back. I want a discipline that sinks deeper than what I have yet experienced." Hecker's impassioned language suggested to his critics a fear of personal freedom and autonomy, values often associated with the Protestant spirit in America. Like Brownson, Hecker was himself critical of Catholic life in America; once he insisted in a letter to Brownson that "a new generation" of leaders must emerge "if Catholicism is to be re-established in the World."

Converts such as Brownson and Hecker enjoyed a great deal of freedom in making careers for themselves as prominent Catholics. Hecker was ordained in England in 1849 as a priest of the Redemptorist order and returned to the United States in 1851 with a small group of fellow American converts intent on evangelizing their countrymen; that is, spreading the "good news" of the Gospels and the teachings of the Catholic Church. In *Questions of the Soul* (1855) and *Aspirations of Nature* (1857), Hecker cited his own experience in arguing that Catholicism was uniquely attuned to a nation that featured both religious freedom and an enduring tradition of personal quests for spiritual fulfillment.

When Hecker made an unauthorized trip to Rome in 1857 seeking papal approval for a new English-speaking mission to the United States under Redemptorist auspices, he was dismissed from the order, but Pope Pius IX subsequently granted Hecker permission to launch a new order, the Congregation of the Missionary Priests of St. Paul the Apostle, or the Paulists. Under Hecker's leadership, the Paulists established an influential parish in New York City, St. Paul the Apostle, while continuing their work in parish missions. The Paulists also directed much of their energies toward evangelizing Protestants. As he explained to a Redemptorist priest in 1848, "I believe that Providence calls me . . . to America to convert a certain class of persons amongst whom I find myself before my conversion." Although the Paulists never succeeded in converting an entire class of people, they helped educate the American public about Catholicism and, inspired by their founder, made a contribution to American spirituality as well. Brownson, Hecker, and other converts promoted an ongoing dialogue between Americans of different faiths; though the exchanges were sometimes contentious, they helped forge a place for Catholics in the American religious landscape.

Isaac Hecker on the Eucharist

Isaac Hecker was a German American from New York who converted to Catholicism in 1844 and subsequently entered the priesthood. In 1858 Hecker and four other fellow American convert priests founded the Missionary Society of St. Paul the Apostle, known as the Paulists. In Questions of the Soul *(1855), he explained the central place of the Eucharist among Catholic sacraments.*

What says Rome to the deep craving of man's heart for love and union with God? The Catholic Church has a full, adequate, and satisfactory answer to this inquiry; an answer that no one can appreciate, unless he already has the highest conception of love.

Love is never satisfied with loving, and is not content until the object loved is wholly in its possession. Love aims always at union.

On the other hand, the object loved is never at rest till it has given itself wholly to its lover. God's love, therefore, for man, cannot be satisfied, until man wholly surrenders himself to God's love; nor can man's love for God be satisfied, until God gives himself entirely to man's love.

God must not only give himself wholly to man, to satisfy his love, but he must give himself in such a way as fitly to be received by man.

The Catholic Church presents to man the Blessed Sacrament as the answer of the deep cry of the soul after love. She tells us, that in Holy Communion is received God entire—the body and blood, the soul and divinity of our Lord Jesus Christ. Christ confirmed this: when instituting the Blessed Sacrament, he said, "Take ye and eat; this is my body. Drink ye all of this; for this is my blood." "He that eateth me, the same also shall live by me." "He that eateth me, the same also shall live by me." "He that eateth my flesh, and drinketh my blood, abideth in me, and I in him."

Besides this, there is another reason why God should give himself to man. It is this; whatever is received as food, must in some way partake of the life it goes to support and sustain; otherwise, starvation and death follow. This is a law of all attraction and life. Now, in the Christian soul, there is a divine life; a divine food, therefore, is necessary for its support, growth, and perfection.

The Catholic Church tells us that we receive this divine food in Holy Communion. Jesus Christ again confirms what she teaches. He says: "Unless you eat the flesh of the Son of man, and drink his blood, you shall have no life in you." "I live by the Father, so he that eateth me, the same also shall live by me."

Thus, the Catholic Saviour is not an abstract Saviour, nor a dead Saviour, separated from us by nineteen centuries, but a real, living, personal Saviour, dwelling in the midst of us, even in our very hearts—our heart's life!

Let those, therefore, who look for, or dream of a "Church of the Future," first learn what the existing and present Church is, and teaches; let them venture to believe her teachings, and dare to obey them. It is a want, on their part, of truthfulness and true courage, to look or ask for what is greater or better, before they know what the present is, and have practised the good it demands.

Chapter 4

Catholic and American

n 1854 a group of Polish immigrants established the community of Panna Marya ("Village of Our Lady") in central Texas. One of the founders of this first permanent settlement of Poles in the United States was Peter Kiolbassa, an 18-year-old native of the small town of Swib, which, with the rest of Poland, was under foreign occupation (in the late 18th and early 19th centuries Poland had been carved up by Russia, Prussia, and Austria-Hungary).

The young Polish-Texan Peter Kiolbassa worked as a cowboy, a waiter, and an elementary-school teacher before enlisting in the Texas cavalry during the Civil War. After being captured by Union troops and taken to Illinois, Kiolbassa switched sides and was quickly made a captain in the U.S. cavalry. In late 1863 he visited Chicago while on furlough and discovered a small Polish-American Catholic community struggling there to establish its first national parish in the rapidly growing city. The following year, with the aid of a Polish priest he knew from Panna Marya, Kiolbassa and several prominent Chicago Poles launched the religious and fraternal Society of St. Stanislaus Kostka, named for Poland's patron saint. Before long Chicago was home to the largest Polish community outside the homeland. By 1918 there were 35 Polish parishes in the Catholic archdiocese of Chicago and the parish of St. Stanislaus Kostka alone contained a staggering 40,000 members, making it the largest parish in America.

A Polish-American congregation gathers in front of the parish church at Bremond, Texas, around 1900. Although Texas was home to the first Polish-American settlement, by the late 19th century most Polish Americans lived in large industrial cities of the Northeast and Midwest.

Polish immigrant Peter Kiolbassa in the uniform of the Union Army. Kiobassa went on to found the St. Stanislaus Kostka Society in Chicago, a group dedicated to the promotion of both Polish and Catholic interests.

The mass migrations of people from eastern and southern Europe in the late 19th century and early 20th centuries dramatically changed American life and reshaped the Catholic Church as well, because a substantial majority of these new Americans flocked to urban parishes created by people like Kiolbassa and other pioneering immigrants. In seeking to preserve their familiar languages and customs, they would challenge an American Catholic establishment—dominated by Irish and, to a lesser extent, German Americans—that had been in place for only a generation. Their communities would also face internal divisions over the fundamental concern of how to embrace the promise of America while remaining faithful to one's homeland, or at least to that remnant of it preserved in the cities of the New World.

Nearly 2 million Poles emigrated to the United States between 1870 and 1920, the great majority of whom were Catholic. Most were farmers uprooted by changes in the agrarian economy provoked by Poland's occupying powers. In the German-ruled territory, for example, 1.25 million acres of land passed out of Polish hands by 1885, although in the Austrian territory the process of industrialization was intentionally delayed to preserve a major source of grain for the Austro-Hungarian Empire. In America, Polish immigrants found grueling, dangerous work in steel mills, coal mines, and meat-packing plants. In addition to Chicago, Polish Catholics established large communities in such industrial cities as Pittsburgh, Buffalo, Baltimore, Milwaukee, and Scranton, Pennsylvania.

Like the Irish before them, the Poles' hopes for survival as a people—in America as in their homeland—were linked to their intense loyalty to the Catholic Church. Polish Catholic spirituality, unaffected by the Protestant Reformation to the west, was marked by a deep devotion to the Blessed Virgin Mary and a total commitment to the local village parish. Like the Irish and the Germans, Polish immigrants in the United States were not comfortable worshiping in parishes led by pastors of a different nationality. In 1870 the Reverend Joseph Dabrowski, a Polish-American priest in Wisconsin, lamented that "our Polish people are living without the Mass, confession, Sunday sermons, and adequate education. Some have settled in the large cities and, because of the lack of priests and the preaching of the word of God, do not attend church services. Without any religious formation, they will certainly be lost to the Church."

By 1870 the leadership of the Catholic Church in the United States was firmly in the grasp of Irish- and German-born bishops, especially in the large cities of the East and Midwest. The Poles and other relatively new immigrant groups found themselves negotiating with these bishops to establish national parishes led by priests from their homeland. In the 1870s in Chicago, for example, Bishop Thomas Foley, an Irish American, granted a Polish religious order—the Congregation of the Resurrection of Our Lord Jesus Christ—the right to administer all Polish-American parishes in the city other than those founded by the diocese itself. The Resurrectionists became a powerful force in Chicago, serving as intermediaries between tens of thousands of Polish immigrants and the diocesan and civil authorities. From their ranks emerged such legendary leaders of the community as the Reverend Vincent Barzynski, pastor of the flagship St. Stanislaus Kostka parish from 1874 until his death in 1899.

The arrangements made between national parishes and bishops, however, often rankled members of Polish fraternal organizations who did not wish to compromise their identities as staunch Polish nationalists in return for legitimacy as American Catholics. The nationalists offered membership in their groups to non-Catholics and nonbelievers while their opponents—sometimes called clericalists—equated Polish identity with Catholicism and were deeply devoted to church organizations like the St. Stanislaus Kostka Society. When nationalist Polish-American organizations in Chicago, Scranton, and Milwaukee challenged the leadership of clerical authorities and sought, as they often did, to establish their own parishes without diocesan approval, the resulting conflicts within these Polish-American communities sometimes resulted in violent clashes between members of rival congregations. In 1896 Francis Hodur, a Polish-American priest in Scranton, organized the Polish National Catholic Church, the only American ethnic church to survive a breakaway from the Roman Catholic Church. Although the great majority of Polish

Americans embraced their diocese-approved clerical leadership, the more militant nationalists raised issues that would be witnessed in many other immigrant communities as well: were they to identify themselves in America as Polish Catholics, Catholic Poles, or simply Polish Americans?

Although Polish Americans became the dominant Catholic immigrant group in several major cities, Italian Americans built an even larger national community, with settlements from New York to San Francisco. In 1857 the first permanent Italian-American parish, St. Mary Magdalen da Pazzi, was founded in Philadelphia. Italian-born missionaries played an important role in building up the church in America, particularly along the western frontier. Joseph Rosati served as bishop of St. Louis from 1826 to 1843 while a Jesuit missionary, Antonio Ravalli, worked among the Native Americans in Montana in the 1840s and 1850s. In 1855 another Jesuit, Gregorio Mengarini, helped found the University of Santa Clara in California.

Prior to the 1870s, however, there were very few Italians living in the United States. Between 1880 and 1900 nearly 1 million Italians emigrated to America: in the two decades that followed, the Italian-American population grew to more than 4 million. Most Italian immigrants came from the economically depressed southern portion of their recently unified homeland. Whether peasant farmers, skilled tradesmen, or unskilled laborers, they all shared an abiding attachment to their village community. Many, if not most, hoped one day to return to Italy.

Like other Catholic immigrant groups, Italians settled primarily in the larger industrialized cities, although some found work in mining regions in the nation's interior. In urban America, Italian immigrants found themselves competing for jobs with well-established groups like the Irish as well as with such fellow newcomers as Jews and Polish Catholics. In New York, Philadelphia, and other eastern cities, the overwhelmingly Catholic Italians were often scorned by Irish and German American priests in whose territorial parishes they had settled; Italians were sometimes even relegated to attending separate masses in church basements.

In 1887 Giovanni Battista Scalabrini, the bishop of Piacenza, Italy, established the Missionaries of St. Charles Borromeo and charged the order to "preserve the Catholic faith in the hearts of our countrymen who have emigrated and to lead them as far as possible to achieve their moral, civil and economic well-being." Bishop Scalabrini encouraged Frances Xavier Cabrini, the Italian-born leader of the Missionary Sisters of the Sacred Heart, to move to the United States in 1889. Mother Cabrini dedicated the remainder of her life to serving Italian immigrants, establishing hospitals, orphanages, and schools across the United States and in South America before dying of malaria in 1917. In 1946 Mother Cabrini became the first American citizen to be declared a saint of the church (Elizabeth Ann Bayley Seton, canonized in 1975, was the first native-born American saint).

Italian Americans cultivated a style of Catholicism that reflected both their European origins and their immigrant experience. Where the Irish invested great spiritual authority in the priesthood, Italian-American spirituality was oriented toward a devotion to family rooted in the peasant villages of the homeland. Italian Americans venerated a concept of the family that was much more complex than our modern-day notions, extended to include those who shared in common the values of the Old World, the ordeal of the immigrant passage, and the crowded tenement life of the new urban village. Patron saints were an intimate part of this family structure: the Italian-American community of East Harlem in New York City, for example, was deeply devoted to Our Lady of Mount Carmel as their protectress long before a church on 115th Street was formally dedicated to her.

The most distinctive feature of Italian-American Catholicism was the *festa,* a devotional celebration originally sponsored by fraternal

Parishioners of St. Francis Church in Lynn, Massachusetts, including servicemen, attach donations to a statue of Mother Cabrini, who had recently been canonized. St. Francis Xavier Cabrini is the patron saint of immigrants.

organizations and later incorporated into parish life. These ritual gatherings presented vivid displays of an Italian-American piety that encompassed not just a church but an entire neighborhood community. Though often dismissed by outsiders as mere street carnivals, the *festa*—usually dedicated to a favored patron saint whose image was held aloft during a procession in the streets—represented a communal reaffirmation of shared bonds of faith and ethnicity.

Italian and Polish immigrants were joined by numerous communities of new immigrants arriving in America between 1865 and 1920. Nearly 1 million French Canadians made the short journey south during this period, attracted by the growing labor market in the textile mills and shoe factories located in such New England towns as Nashua, New Hampshire, and Lowell, Massachusetts. Like the Poles and the Irish, the French Canadians linked their survival as a people to an enduring loyalty to the Catholic Church.

Other predominantly Catholic immigrant groups of the late 19th and early 20th centuries included Slovaks, Czechs (generally known at the time as Bohemians), Lithuanians, and Ukrainians. Although the various Catholic immigrant communities differed from one another in significant ways, they shared certain general characteristics. Originating almost entirely from either rural areas or small towns, these new immigrants usually became urban-dwelling Americans. Where most had identified themselves as citizens of a village or, at most, a region within an ill-defined European nation-state, they found themselves labeled in America not as Sicilians or Galicians but simply as Italians or Poles. Eventually, immigrants came to identify themselves in this manner as well, because the urban "villages" they created in the midst of large cities attracted settlers from different regions of their homelands. In the process of becoming "ethnic" Americans, newcomers learned that it was best to put local differences of origin aside in the name of a more communal solidarity.

Along the southern border of the United States, Catholicism had flourished on Mexican soil for centuries prior to the birth of the United States, and a substantial Mexican population lived in territories annexed by the United States following the Mexican War of 1846–48. The first

Mexican Americans were not immigrants but a conquered people with deep roots in a territory in which they suddenly found themselves treated as "foreigners." Mexicans who later emigrated to the southwestern United States were readily integrated into a Hispanic community that strongly resisted efforts by both the civil and church authorities to enforce assimilation into unfamiliar patterns of social and religious life. The first bishops of Texas, New Mexico, and California—all of whom were European-born—removed Mexican pastors from their parishes and failed to encourage vocations to the priesthood within members of the local community, importing instead Irish, French, German, Italian, and Spanish priests.

The traditions of Mexican Catholicism persisted despite the misgivings of American church leaders, just as they had in the period of Spanish rule. A case in point is the parish of San Fernando, which was established in San Antonio, Texas, in 1731, more than a century before Texas achieved statehood. After the United States assumed permanent control of the region, San Fernando became the focal point of Mexican Americans' efforts to maintain their spiritual and cultural identity in the San Antonio area. A U.S. soldier noted that the altar of the church was adorned with "a wooden figure of a Mexican representing Christ on the cross." Even when Mexican priests were removed from the parish in the 1840s, San Fernando remained the site of annual celebrations in honor of Our Lady of Guadalupe, the patroness of the Mexican people. (In 1531 the Blessed Virgin Mary had appeared before a young Indian man, Juan Diego, in a village near Mexico City. The Basilica of Our Lady Guadalupe was built near the site of the apparition and continues to attract millions of pilgrims each year.) In 1874 San Fernando was designated the cathedral of the new diocese of San Antonio.

Mexican-American girls pose before a crucifix adorned with roses at a ceremony marking their first reception of the sacrament of Holy Communion. The ceremony took place in Arizona around 1900.

83

Celebrants of the Feast of Our Lady of Guadalupe emerge from San Fernando Cathedral in San Antonio, Texas, on December 12, 1933. The annual festival attracts the faithful from many parts of Southwest Texas and continues to be a focal point of Mexican-American spirituality in the San Antonio area.

The new Catholic communities of the late 19th century differed from each other in important respects, but they each experienced a tension akin to that of the Polish Americans' struggle between those who defined their identity primarily in terms of a new commitment to the church in America and those who wished to maintain a stronger connection to the spiritual and cultural traditions of the homeland. This inherent conflict was not limited to new immigrants, however; the entire Catholic Church in the United States became embroiled in an "Americanist controversy" in the late 19th century.

The Americanist controversy pitted a group of largely Irish-American moderately liberal, or "Americanist," bishops against a coalition of Irish and German-American conservative bishops who feared that as Catholics became more Americanized they would surrender their unique spiritual traditions and imperil their souls. The Americanists believed that Catholicism was fully compatible with national traditions and democratic institutions.

A series of issues emerging in the 1880s set the stage for bitter conflict. Some conservative bishops wished to see Catholics banned from participation in the Knights of Labor, a growing national labor union, because it allegedly resembled a "secret society" akin to the Freemasons (a fraternal organization founded in 18th-century England that was hostile to Catholicism) and other traditional enemies of the church. Although the bishop of Quebec won Vatican condemnation of the Knights in Canada in 1884, the American bishops rejected that option by a vote of 10 to 2. The Knights achieved their greatest U.S. prominence under the leadership of Terence Powderly, a Catholic machinist who was elected grand master in 1879 and helped convince the bishops that union membership was not incompatible with loyalty to the church.

The Irish-American bishops who most energetically defended the Knights of Labor—James Gibbons of Baltimore, John J. Keane of Richmond, and John Ireland of St. Paul—were the leaders of the Americanist wing of the church hierarchy, though Gibbons was also a national Catholic leader with ties to all factions of the church. Ireland's family had fled the Irish potato famine in 1849 when he was 11 years old. They made their way to St. Paul, Minnesota, where the French-born bishop of that tiny frontier diocese quickly recognized the young immigrant's scholastic gifts and sent him to a French seminary in 1853. Ireland was ordained to the priesthood in 1861 and served with great distinction as a chaplain for Minnesota's Union troops. After the war, while still in his twenties, he became a leader in the American Catholic temperance movement, which sought to curtail alcohol abuse, and launched a program to resettle Irish immigrants on Minnesota farmland. Ireland was named bishop of St. Paul in 1884.

Terence Powderly worked with James Cardinal Gibbons of Baltimore to win the church's approval of Catholic workers' participation in the Knights of Labor. *Frank Leslie's Illustrated Newspaper* from October 1886 depicts Powderly (center) at the Tenth Annual Convention of the Knights of Labor.

VIRGINIA.—TENTH ANNUAL CONVENTION OF THE KNIGHTS OF LABOR AT RICHMOND—FRANK J. FARRELL, COLORED DELEGATE OF DISTRICT ASSEMBLY NO. 49, INTRODUCING GENERAL MASTER WORKMAN POWDERLY TO THE CONVENTION.

The nation's Roman Catholic bishops met at the Third Plenary Council in Baltimore in 1884. The 72 bishops in attendance included leaders of such new western dioceses as Santa Fe, New Mexico (1853, founded); Leavenworth, Kansas (1877); and Helena, Montana (1884).

That same year, at the Third Plenary Council of Baltimore, the American bishops asserted their desire for "every Catholic child in the land" to have "the benefit of a Catholic school." The bishops mandated the establishment of a Catholic grammar school in every parish within two years. School construction was a costly process borne for the most part by individual parishes, and the church's leaders differed over the proper means to fulfill this mandate.

John Ireland, who had long been an admirer of U.S. public schools, was even invited to address the National Education Association when it met in St. Paul in 1890. Knowing that fewer than half of all Catholic children attended parochial (parish)schools, which generally charged a modest tuition, Ireland devised a plan by which the state would fund the operation of Catholic schools, with religious instruction provided after regular school hours. Bishop Frederick Katzer of Milwaukee and other conservatives in the church were outraged by Ireland's scheme, believing it would result in state control over Catholic religious education.

When Bishop Ireland's plan was adopted in two Minnesota communities, he sought Vatican approval for this novel solution to the problem of Catholic schooling. Ireland won support for his plan from faculty members at the newly created Catholic University of America in Washington, D.C. In turn, that school's rector, the Americanist John J. Keane, gave Ireland an important role in directing the fledgling institution. Ireland and the Americanists won a great victory in 1893 when Pope Leo XIII urged local bishops to determine the best arrangements for Catholic schooling in their dioceses, though the Minnesota experiment ultimately fell victim to conflicts between Catholics and Protestants.

Between 1880 and 1900 enrollment in Catholic elementary schools increased from 405,000 students to more than 1.23 million, but since the overall Catholic population increased at a similar rate, it is clear that parents appreciated the option of sending their children either to public or parochial schools. One reason for the widespread acceptance of Catholic elementary schools was that the presence in them of teaching sisters from more than 40 communities of religious women ensured that the schools would be staffed by pious and conscientious teachers. The nationwide system of Catholic schools that resulted came to represent one of the greatest achievements in U.S. religious history.

A charismatic New York priest, Edward McGlynn, was among a relatively small number of Catholic clergymen who openly favored public schools over parochial institutions. A product of public elementary schools, he felt that the church should concentrate on religious instruction instead of spending enormous sums on schools. McGlynn became even more controversial in 1886 when he defied a ban by his conservative archbishop, Michael A. Corrigan, and campaigned vigorously on behalf of New York mayoral candidate Henry George, a radical reformer. George was best known for his advocacy of a steep tax on property owners. Since their wealth in land and buildings was enhanced by the toil of poorly paid workers, he argued, property owners must be obliged to share the proceeds of rising values. Many New Yorkers, including Archbishop Corrigan, viewed George's scheme as an attack on the right to own private property.

Father McGlynn was a fiery preacher and champion of the oppressed. In an interview with a reporter McGlynn expressed his disdain for "ministers of the Gospel and priests of the Church [who] tell the hardworking poor to be content with their lot and hope for good times in heaven." Archbishop Corrigan promptly suspended Father McGlynn, who was later excommunicated (banned from administering or receiving the sacraments, but not expelled from the church) after refusing a summons to appear in Rome and explain himself. In 1892 Italian Archbishop Francesco Satolli, who was visiting the United States as papal delegate to the Columbian Exposition in Chicago, restored McGlynn to the good graces of the church. Father McGlynn subsequently resumed his priestly career in Newburgh, New York. The ensuing furor deeply divided the Catholic Church in America, especially after Archbishop Corrigan grew convinced that Cardinal Gibbons of Baltimore had intervened with the Vatican on McGlynn's behalf.

Although all the key figures on both sides of the McGlynn conflict were of Irish descent, the Americanist controversy was aggravated by ethnic discord between Irish and German Americans. In 1883 a German Catholic politician, Peter Paul Cahensly, visited the United States on behalf of the St. Raphael Society, an organization dedicated to aiding immigrants from the homeland. Cahensly, along with other prominent Germans, feared that his Catholic countrymen were being mistreated by the church in America. In 1891 Cahensly delivered to Pope Leo XIII a document known as the Lucerne Memorial, which alleged that "more than ten million souls" had been lost to the church in the period of mass migration, an exaggerated figure by any measure. The report called for establishing more national parishes and schools and furnishing a more ethnically diverse pool of candidates for the U.S. hierarchy, which was derisively termed by some the "hibernarchy," due to the preponderance of Irish-American bishops (Ireland had once been known as Hibernia).

Cardinal Gibbons of Baltimore objected to this interference in U.S. Catholic affairs by "officious gentlemen" in Europe and preached a sermon in which he promised: "We will prove to our countrymen that the ties formed by grace and faith are stronger than flesh and blood. God and our country—this [is] our watchword. Loyalty to God's church and to our country—this [is] our religious and political faith." Cardinal Gibbons, the most influential member of the U.S. hierarchy, was congratulated for his patriotism by President Benjamin Harrison at a vacation meeting in Cape May, New Jersey, in July 1892. The Vatican initially took the middle ground in the conflict, rejecting the recommendations of the Lucerne Memorial but acknowledging the desires of non-Irish ethnic groups for clergy and bishops from their own communities. The church moved slowly: the first Polish-American bishop, for example, was not installed until 1908.

The Americanists were encouraged in 1893 when Archbishop Francesco Satolli, the Vatican's newly appointed permanent apostolic delegate (or papal representative) to the United States, exhorted the audience attending a Catholic congress at the Chicago World's Fair to go forth "in one hand bearing the book of Christian truth and in the other the Constitution of the United States." Satolli disapproved, however, of the participation of Cardinal Gibbons and Archbishop Ireland in the World Parliament of Religions, an event held at the fairgrounds that brought together not only Protestant, Catholic, and Jewish leaders but Hindus, Moslems, and Buddhists as well. Satolli was also surprised to discover that many U.S. bishops opposed John Ireland's liberal policies on Catholic education to the degree that by 1896 he had reversed his position and become a staunch foe of the Americanists.

The final act in the Americanism controversy began in 1898 with the publication in France of Paulist priest Walter Elliot's 1891 biography of Isaac Hecker, founder of the Paulists. A French priest, Abbé Felix Klein, translated an abridged French version, which included Archbishop John Ireland's introduction from the original addition as well as a preface by Abbé Klein himself. Klein admired the innovations associated with Ireland

James Cardinal Gibbons served as archbishop of Baltimore from 1877 to 1921 and was the acknowledged leader of the American church hierarchy for most of that period. *Columbia* magazine, which celebrated its 50th anniversary in 1882, is an official publication of the Knights of Columbus.

Pope Leo XIII reigned from 1878 to 1903. His 1891 encyclical *Rerum Novarum* ("On the Condition of the Working Classes") launched a new tradition of Catholic social thought, but his 1899 condemnation of "Americanism" was based on faulty information from European sources.

and other American church leaders, but conservative French Catholics responded to his translation by condemning what they called "Americanism" as a form of disloyalty to the pope.

The hostility of many European Catholics to American civilization was heightened by the Spanish-American War of 1898, which ended Spanish control over Cuba and saw the United States acquire Puerto Rico and the Philippines, formerly Spanish possessions. This "splendid little war," as it was described by Secretary of State John Hay, was viewed by many Americans as a triumph of Anglo-Saxon Protestantism over a decadent European Catholic nation. In January 1899, Leo XIII addressed a papal letter to Cardinal Gibbons, *Testem Benevolentiae* ("Witness to Good Will"), in which he avoided direct accusation but noted certain alleged characteristics of Americanism which, if true, were deemed unacceptable.

The pope cited as erroneous all arguments that the church should adapt itself to the modern world, lessen its rigors in order to attract more converts, and encourage the cultivation of personal spirituality at the expense of external authority. Although the pope distinguished these charges from "the characteristic qualities which reflect honor on the people of America," his letter had a chilling effect on American Catholics who wished to further explore the common ground shared by their faith community and American democracy.

Regardless of Rome's view of the affair, the Americanism controversy showed that there was more than one way to envision Catholic life in the United States. The opponents of Americanism were not necessarily un-American at all. Many of the leaders of the Polish nationalist movement in the United States, for example, were lay men and women who believed that the persistence of a strong Polish identity did not disqualify them as Americans, though it did put them in conflict with Polish-Catholic religious leaders who stressed the virtues of accommodation with the American church. The broad variety of ways in which immigrant peoples created religious communities signified the real triumph of Catholic Americanism.

The late 19th century witnessed a dramatic shift in the focus of American life as the rural and small-town civilization that had prevailed for so long was finally overtaken by the growing concentrations in the cities, especially those in the Northeast and Midwest. Because the majority of Catholic immigrants were found in those cities, and because urban life was in a state of great flux throughout the period, newcomers suffered fewer disadvantages than they would have in more established communities.

Irish Americans were only the first Catholic immigrant group to enjoy great prominence in an expanding urban culture. Many Irishmen arrived in their new urban environments with little more than a command of English and a less tangible but equally important appreciation for the structures of authority that bound people together in communities. These attributes were highly valuable in ethnically and religiously diverse American cities whose social and political boundaries were being redrawn under the pressure of massive immigration. Highly loyal to the Democratic party, Irish Americans dominated many urban political "machines" after 1870. William R. Grace was elected the first Irish-American mayor of New York City in 1880, not long after the Irish assumed control of Tammany Hall, the Democratic organization that dominated New York politics and government.

Colorful Tammany Hall election precinct bosses such as George Washington Plunkitt symbolized the increasing political influence of Irish Americans. Plunkitt's duties, as he explained in his memoir *Plunkitt of Tammany Hall,* included attending weddings and funerals of constituents of all faiths, obtaining licenses for street vendors, finding shelter for victims of fires, and providing bail for prisoners. The political machines were organized in a hierarchical fashion that some people compared to the structure of the Catholic Church, but if the party bosses did often perform charitable works, they clearly perceived politics as a business from which they expected to profit. Although the political machines and the church occupied separate if occasionally overlapping spheres in urban America, Protestant reformers often linked them as twin evils. In 1884 a group of ministers assured Republican presidential candidate James G.

The immensely popular John L. Sullivan, "the Boston Strong Boy," won the heavyweight boxing title by defeating one fellow Irish American (Paddy Ryan) in 1882 and lost it at the fists of another ("Gentleman Jim" Corbett) in 1892.

Blaine in New York that "we are Republicans and don't propose to leave our party, and identify ourselves with the party whose antecedents have been rum, Romanism [Catholicism] and rebellion." Blaine lost the election to Grover Cleveland; politicians with aspirations for national office learned not to antagonize urban Catholic voters.

In the late 19th century the urban Irish became increasingly identified with a buoyant, rakish style whose appeal transcended religious and ethnic boundaries. Big-city newspapers chronicled the exploits of such folk heroes as John "Old Smoke" Morrisey, who won the U.S. heavyweight boxing championship in 1853 and went on to amass a great fortune, serve in Congress, and establish a fashionable gambling salon at Saratoga Springs, New York.

Sports were among the primary vehicles of Catholic aspiration in America. John L. Sullivan, an Irish-American prizefighter who studied briefly with the Jesuits at Boston College, became a national hero in the 1880s, when he reigned as heavyweight champion. He once exclaimed, "There's enough Sullivans to make an army big enough to capture Canada from the British and make it Irish, like it ought to be." Yet during a triumphant tour of England in 1887, he informed the Prince of Wales: "I'm proud to meet you. If you ever come to Boston be sure to look me up; I'll see that you're treated right."

Urban Catholics recognized that success in sports was a means to greater national acceptance at a time when they were still excluded from many occupations. As late as 1912 an Irish-American newspaper could report that the presence of Irish-born athletes competing for the U.S. Olympic team was "a matter of self-gratulation to Irishman," refuting "many of the ignorant calumnies cast upon us by our enemies, who have tried to depict us as a debauched and inferior race."

Journalism was another field in which Irish-American Catholics bridged the gulf between their community and the broader world of the urban metropolis. One of the best-known and respected journalists of the era was Finley Peter Dunne, who became editorial-page managing editor of the *Chicago Evening Post* in 1892 at the age of 26. A year later Dunne unveiled one of the most memorable characters in American literature, Martin J. Dooley, a fictitious Chicago saloonkeeper through whom Dunne presented some of the wit and wisdom of Irish-American vernacular speech.

Mr. Dooley offered his opinions from a vantage point deep in the Irish-American enclave of Bridgeport, on Chicago's South Side, but he spoke to Chicagoans of all backgrounds and ultimately—once Dunne's columns were reprinted in book form—to the entire nation. Where Irish-American dialect had often been the butt of jokes, Dunne captured the flavor and the ethos of urban-immigrant life with insight and compassion. Mr. Dooley often paid tribute to parish priests, including a Father Kelly who, he noted in a column from 1897, "spint all th' money that he ought to be usin' to buy a warm coat f'r his back, spint it on th' poor, an he dipt into th' Easter colliction that ought to've gone to pay interest in th' church morgedge. It'll be a smooth talk he'll have to give his grace th' archbishop this year." Mr. Dooley also vividly described a parish fair, one

Irish-American domestic workers were depicted as "Happy Laundry Girls" in an 1891 advertisement for Kirkman's Borax Soap. Though the advertisement traded on an ethnic stereotype, the use of Catholic immigrants to sell consumer goods was a novel idea at the time.

of the most popular institutions of Irish-American life: "They had Roddy's Hibernyun band playin' on th' corner an' th' basement iv the church was packed. In the back they had a shootin' gall'ry where ye got five shots f'r tin cints . . . The booths was something iligant. Mrs. Dorsey had th' first wan where she sold mottoes an' babies' clothes."

Although his uncle was the pastor of a prominent Irish-American church in Chicago, Finley Peter Dunne attended public schools and was not active in the church as an adult. His eldest sister, Amelia Dunne Hookway,

Mr. Dooley on Lent

Finley Peter Dunne was a renowned humorist who created the fictional character Martin J. Dooley while working as a columnist for the Chicago Evening Post *in 1893. While other journalists had employed demeaning caricatures of "stage Irishmen" to reinforce stereotypes about Irish Americans, Dunne's compelling essays revealed the unique qualities of urban-Irish neighborhood life, lightheartedly addressing issues of great importance. The 40-day period (not counting Sundays) prior to Easter is known as Lent, a time of prayer and fasting. Pastors of Irish-American parishes often supplied "dispensations" for St. Patrick's Day, enabling parishioners to forego Lenten sacrifices in order to celebrate the feast of their patron saint. This custom provides the backdrop for Dunne's gently satirical essay.*

"O-HO," said Mr. Hennessy, "twenty-wan days to Saint Patrick's day."

"Ar-re ye keepin' Lent?" asked Mr. Dooley.

"I am," said Mr. Hennessy. "I put th' pipe back iv th' clock day befure yisterdah night. Oh, but th' las' whiff iv th' ol clay was plisint. Ar-re ye keepin' Lent?"

"I am that," said Mr. Dooley. "I'm on'y smokin' me seegars half through, an' I take no sugar in me tay. Th' Lord give me stren'th to last till Pathrick's day! I'm keepin' Lent, but I'm not goin' up an' down the sthreet tellin' people about it. I ain't anny produer iv keepin' Lent thin I am iv keepin' clean. In our fam'ly we've always kept it. I raymimber seein' me father tuck away th' pipe, cork up th' bottle an' put it in a thrunk with something between a moan and a cheer, an' begin to find fault with th' wurruld. F'r us kids Lent was no gr-reat hardship. It on'y meant not enough iv something besides meat. I don't raymimber much about it exceipt that on Ash Winsdah ivrybody had a smudge on his forehead; an afther awhile th' house begun to smell a little iv fish, an about th' thirtieth day th' eggs had thrown off all disguise an' was just plain, yellow eggs. . . .

I don't expict Father Kelly will sind down th' Father Macchew Fife an' Dhrum Corps to serenade me because I left that lump iv sugar out iv me tay an' put in twice as much milk. . . . No, sire, I congrathylate mesilf on me sthrong will power, an' reyflict that sugar makes people fat. I am niver goin' to place anny medals on anny wan f'r bein' varchous, Hinnissy, f'r if varchue ain't always necissity, me boy, its th' next thing to it. I'm tim'prate because too much dhrink doesn't agree with me; modest because I look best that way; gin'rous because I don't want to be thought stingy; honest because iv th' polis force; an' brave whin I can't r-run away.

"Dock Grogan, who's an ol' pagan, don't agree with Father Kelly on more thin two things, though they're th' frindliest iv inimies; an' wan iv thim is Lent. Father Kelly says 'tis good f'r th' soul, an' Dock Grogan he says 'tis good f'r th' body. It comes at th' r-right time iv th' year, he says, whin ivrybody had had a winther iv stuffin' thimsilves an' floodin' their inteeryors an' settin' up late at night. It's a kind iv a stand off f'r th' Chris'mas holidays. We quit atin' meat because 'tis Lent—an we've had too much meat. We quit smokin' because 'tis Lent—an' we have a smokers' heart. We quit dhrink because it's Lent—and we want to see if th' brakes ar-re wurrukin'. We quit goin' to th' theaytres because it's Lent—an' we're sick iv th' theaytres. If it wasn't f'r Lent in March none iv us wud live till th' Fourth iv July. 'In Lent,' says Father Kelly, 'I get me congregation back.' 'In Lent,' says Dock Grogan, 'I lose mine.' 'Lent,' says Father Kelly, 'brings thim nearer Hiven.' 'An longer away,' says Dock Grogan. 'It's hard wurruk f'r me, but I like it,' says Father Kelly. 'It's my vacation time,' says Dock Grogan, 'but I don't care f'r it.' 'It makes thim think iv th' next wurruld,' says Father Kelly. 'An' gives thim a betther hold on this,' says Dock Grogan. 'It's rellijon,' says Father Kelly. 'It's med'cine,' says Dock Grogan.

"So I say, no medals, plaze, f'r me on account iv that lump iv sugar. I done me jooty an' no more. Whin th' divvle timpted me to put in th' lump I said: 'Get thee behind me, Satan, I'm too fat now.' That was all. I done what was r-right, because it was r-right and pious an' a good thing f'r me to do. I don't claim no gratichood. I don't ask f'r anny admiration iv me piety. But don't I look betther, Hinnissy? Don't ye see I'm a little thinner?"

"Not an inch," said Mr. Hennessy. "Ye're th' same hippypotymus ye was."

"Well, well," said Mr. Dooley. "That's sthrange. P'raps I'm a betther man, afther all. How long did ye say it was to Pathrick's day?"

attended parochial schools before enjoying a highly distinguished career as a public school educator. By 1910, more than one-third of the public school teachers in Chicago, Boston, and several other large cities were Irish-American women. A backlash finally ensued: Professor Loftus D. Coleman of Columbia University Teachers College complained in 1911 of the growing "problem of teachers who are not thoroughly Americanized," while a University of Chicago professor warned that a majority of teachers in that city "look to the Vatican for guidance." Female Irish-American teachers looked instead to their own urban immigrant experience as a unique resource in ethnically and religiously diverse classrooms. Amelia Dunne Hookway and many other female Catholic teachers served as intermediaries between immigrant families and urban public schools. Their insight and sensitivity helped to ease their students through the often difficult process of "Americanization" that was a central mission of public education.

Between 1910 and 1930, a new generation of church leaders grew determined that the Catholic schools should perform a similar function. As the controversies within the church over "Americanism" receded into the past, such big-city archbishops as William Henry O'Connell of Boston, Dennis Dougherty of Philadelphia, and George Mundelein of Chicago confidently built enormous, well-organized systems of parish schools in their dioceses. The number of children attending Catholic schools increased from around 400,000 in 1880 to 1.7 million in 1920 (the overall Catholic population during the same period grew from roughly 7.5 million to 19 million). Catholic High School of Philadelphia, founded in 1890, was the first secondary school sponsored by an American diocese. Many more Catholic high schools were built in the first two decades of the 20th century, reflecting a movement first proposed by leaders in public education, who viewed secondary schools as "people's colleges," since very few students would go on to pursue a higher education.

Changes in Catholic higher education similarly reflected broader developments in the late 19th and early 20th centuries. Nearly all of the American colleges founded before the Civil War were affiliated with churches. Most of the colleges founded by Catholic religious orders in the mid-19th century (such as St. Joseph's College, founded by Jesuits in Philadelphia in 1851, or St. Bonaventure College, founded by Franciscan friars in Olean, New York, in 1858) offered both college preparatory and college-level courses of instruction. By the end of the 19th century, however, many of the most prominent colleges founded by Protestant churches (such as Yale and Princeton) were well on their way to becoming largely secular institutions focusing on research and graduate programs as well as undergraduate education. This "university movement"—heavily influenced by developments in German higher education—greatly influenced the development of the Catholic University of America, founded in 1887.

Catholic University focused on graduate programs in such fields as theology and education and most of its students were seminarians or members of religious communities. Other Catholic colleges whose students were primarily interested in careers outside of the church were gradually transformed into universities in the early decades of the 20th century. Most of these institutions (such as Saint Louis University, Marquette University in Milwaukee, and Fordham University in the Bronx, New York) were located in major urban centers and produced many of the leading figures of their communities in such fields as law and politics. While enrollment in undergraduate programs at Catholic universities was generally restricted to men, their graduate programs attracted students from many of the women's colleges that were founded early in the 20th century by women's religious communities. The College of St. Catherine, founded in 1905 in St. Paul, Minnesota, by the Sisters of St. Joseph of Carondelet, and the College of New Rochelle, founded that same year by Ursuline sisters in a suburb of New York City, were just two among many women's colleges that quickly gained prominence in Catholic higher education. Graduates of Catholic colleges and universities would play important roles in the many campaigns for social reform launched in the first three decades of the 20th century.

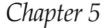
Chapter 5

Reformers and Crusaders

American society has frequently witnessed a strong impulse toward reform of its major institutions. The Progressive era (stretching roughly from the late 1890s until 1917, when the United States entered World War I) and the New Deal years of the depression-wracked 1930s were two periods marked by sustained desires to achieve greater social and economic justice in the United States. Because so much of the reform activity of the Progressive era and the New Deal focused on urban life, American Catholics found themselves closer to the center of national concerns than ever before. Throughout these periods, the church was also involved in a campaign for greater organization and effectiveness that mirrored national trends.

In a pastoral letter of 1884, the American bishops urged "every hand among the people of God" to share in the work of "building up the 'spiritual house,' the tabernacle of God with men. " One component of the bishops' ambitious strategy of mobilization was the formation of the lay Catholic Congress, which first convened in Baltimore in 1889. This meeting and a second Congress held in Chicago in 1893 signaled the emergence of lay people organized to work on behalf of the church. Delegates to the 1889 Congress resolved to "cooperate with the clergy in discussing and in solving those great economic and social questions which affect the interests and well-being of the church, the country, and society at large." The members of the Catholic Congress wished to "show to our fellow

One hundred fifty thousand people attended a mass at Chicago's Soldier Field during the 1926 International Eucharistic Congress, the first gathering of its kind held in the United States. The event demonstrated the great devotion of Catholics to the sacrament of the Eucharist and also showcased the growth of the church in America.

countrymen the true relations that exist between the church that we obey and love, and the government of our choice."

"This is an age of organization and concentration," wrote James A. McFaul, the bishop of Trenton, New Jersey, in a 1904 article promoting the American Federation of Catholic Societies, which had been founded three years earlier. The Federation also aimed to reduce the exclusively ethnic character of many existing fraternal organizations serving immigrants. McFaul described these immigrants as having "settled down like an immense flock of migrating birds. . . . The friction resulting from association with other races will gradually disintegrate these colonies, and their members will sooner or later be merged into and assimilated by the general population of the nation."

The Knights of Columbus, founded in New Haven, Connecticut, in 1882 by a young priest named Michael McGivney, symbolized the transition of Catholic fraternal organizations from local and ethnic to national and inclusive. Although the Knights of Columbus was dominated by Irish Americans, the organization was open to all Catholic men in good standing with the church; by 1914 membership in the Knights exceeded 300,000. Like many non-Catholic fraternal organizations, the Knights of Columbus offered a low-cost life insurance program that heightened its appeal. The Knights provided fellowship while sponsoring ambitious public education campaigns designed to combat the lingering forces of anti-Catholicism.

The growing desire within the church to consolidate its membership while reaching out to the broader society was reflected in the work of a leading Progressive-era Catholic reformer, Father Peter E. Dietz. Dietz sought to unite his German-American constituency with the larger community of American Catholic labor and reform organizations. "We have had language, church and school problems," he acknowledged in 1907 in the journal of a German-American organization. "We have had a large share of the problem of adding another province to the commonwealth of the Church Universal, laying out the territory, clearing away the wilderness of prejudice and antipathy and breaking a new soil from behind the Catholic plough. These problems have largely been solved, and with all

the good-will in the world and with all the rock-ribbed conviction of the Catholic faith in our hearts we turn with enthusiasm to the newer problems of social legislation." In 1910
Dietz organized the Militia of Christ for Social Service, a
group of Catholic trade unionists that worked to strengthen
links between the church and the labor movement.

In an age of reform, a young priest-scholar emerged as the
leading Catholic voice in the quest for social justice. John A.
Ryan was born in rural Minnesota in 1869, one of 11 children
in an immigrant family from County Tipperary, Ireland. As a
boy Ryan absorbed the spirit of midwestern populism, a
movement that fought for farmers' rights and against monop-
olies, the control of entire industries by a single corporation.
Educated at public and Catholic schools and ordained in St.
Paul, Minnesota, Ryan was sent by Archbishop John Ireland to study at
the Catholic University of America in Washington, D.C., in 1898. Deeply
interested in the relationship between economic and social issues and
Catholic thought, in 1906 he published *A Living Wage,* the first attempt
by an American to apply the lessons of Pope Leo XIII's celebrated 1891
encyclical *Rerum Novarum* (known in the English-speaking world by various titles, including "On the Condition of the Working Classes"). *Rerum
Novarum* served notice that the church was deeply concerned with social
issues and was determined to foster a Catholic social doctrine that was
applicable throughout the world.

Ryan echoed the pope in asserting that all workers had a moral right
to a living wage rooted in their God-given dignity as human beings.
Employers, he argued, now bore the "obligation of providing" workers
"with the material means of living decently"; it was also the duty of the
state to ensure that all workers were justly compensated for their labor.
In 1909 Ryan wrote a two-part article for the Paulist Fathers' *Catholic
World* magazine in which he outlined legislative proposals for minimum-
wage laws, an eight-hour day, provisions for public housing, and government programs to support the unemployed, the elderly, and the disabled.
He also called for the enactment of many of the reforms demanded by

Father John A. Ryan began
teaching at the Catholic
University of America in
1915 and soon established
himself as the nation's
leading Catholic social
thinker. In 1935 he was
director of the National
Catholic Welfare Confer-
ence—Social Action
Department.

populists and progressives, including government ownership of railroads and public utilities.

In his 1941 book *Social Doctrine in Action,* Ryan recalled that early in his career he "found only a handful of Catholics who were prominent" in reform activities that reached beyond the boundaries of the church: "Intelligent and competent Catholics were willing to work for laudable objectives in a Catholic organization, but seemed timid or fearful about associating with non-Catholics for similar purposes." While the Americanists of the late 19th century had stressed the compatibility of Catholicism and American life and stressed the positive aspects of national life, John A. Ryan helped lead the church in a new direction. His pioneering work made possible a clear Catholic response to the injustices that accompanied the rapid urbanization and industrialization of the United States.

The American bishops staunchly supported the nation's intervention in World War I; in 1917 they established the National Catholic War Council to coordinate the church's role in the war effort, which centered around the establishment of Catholic visitors' centers in military training camps and the assignment of chaplains and social service workers to duty near the front lines of battle in Europe. In 1919 the bishops established the National Catholic Welfare Council (renamed the National Catholic Welfare Conference in 1923) partly as a vehicle for the bishops' pronouncements on social issues. While the American bishops were not fully in accord with John A. Ryan's philosophy, in 1919 as a sign of their respect for his reformist zeal they invited him to draft *The Bishops' Program of Social Reconstruction.* Ryan's document called for both political and spiritual reforms and warned that governmental regulation of the social order was no substitute for religious renewal. "Changes in our economic and political systems," Ryan wrote for the Bishops' Program, "will have only partial and feeble efficiency if they be not reinforced by the Christian view of work and wealth." Ryan promoted the traditional Catholic view that small-scale, voluntary initiatives focusing on the family and religious communities were always preferable to impersonal governmental programs.

Some critics, Catholic and non-Catholic alike, found Ryan's work highly controversial, and the Bishops' Program was even called socialistic by more than a few critics, who felt that the church had no business meddling in economic matters. On the other hand, the crusading author Upton Sinclair called the program a "Catholic miracle," because it undermined the view held by many secular reformers that the church had no interest in issues of social justice (and because Sinclair was unaware of the 1891 encyclical *Rerum Novarum* that had inspired the Bishops' Program). The booming economy of the 1920s drove reformers like Ryan into temporary obscurity. But his work was indirectly responsible, at the very least, for a broadened perspective among Catholic public servants who came of age in the early years of the 20th century.

Alfred E. Smith was the best known and one of the most colorful American Catholic politicians of the 20th century's first three decades. Born in 1873, Al Smith grew up in an Irish-American neighborhood on the Lower East Side of Manhattan, though in addition to his Irish roots Smith also had English, German, and possibly Italian ancestors. He left school at the age of 15, not long after the death of his father. Smith liked to say that he held a degree from the Fulton Fish Market, where he worked to help support his mother and younger sister. He was an active member of his parish church, where he developed his oratorical skills in numerous theatrical productions. Like so many other Irish Americans in New York, Smith was a loyal member of his local Democratic party club. He diligently worked his way up through the ranks of the party organization and was rewarded in 1895 with a job in the Jury Commissioner's office for a weekly salary of $16.

In 1903, Smith was elected to the New York State Assembly and quickly rose to join the hierarchy of the statewide party. In addition to his

During the First World War, the Knights of Columbus established a Three Million Dollar War Fund to provide religious activities for Catholics and recreational facilities for all servicemen in training camps. A joint drive with the Y.M.C.A., the Jewish Welfare Board, and the Salvation Army raised more than $30 million for the Knights' War Camp Fund.

Delegates committed to the candidacy of Alfred E. Smith demonstrate their support at the 1928 Democratic National Convention in Houston, Texas. Smith, the highly popular governor of New York State, easily won the nomination but was trounced in the general election by Republican Herbert Hoover.

gift for public speaking, Smith was a shrewd, well-organized politician who enjoyed the details of legislative work. He fought for many of the reforms championed by John A. Ryan while remaining a most practical politician keenly aware of the necessity of compromise. In 1911, after almost 150 women were killed in a fire at the Triangle Shirtwaist factory in New York City, Smith was named vice-chairman of an investigative committee appointed by the state legislature. He toured factories and sweatshops where women and children—many of them immigrants—endured inhumane conditions, prompting him to remark: "We have been in a great hurry to legislate for the interests . . . [But] we have been slow to legislate along the direction that means thanksgiving to the poorest man in history—to Him who was born in a stable in Bethlehem."

Like many other urban Catholics of the early 20th century, Smith learned to appreciate the ethnic and religious diversity of his surroundings. His quest for social justice brought him in contact with professional social workers and other reformers who were viewed with great suspicion by many in New York's Irish-dominated Tammany Hall. Smith broadened his own horizons and those of his constituents without surrendering allegiance to the tightly controlled political organization. Belle Moskowitz, a Jewish woman with a background in social work, labor arbitration, and the woman suffrage movement (which sought voting rights for women), became his most valued advisor. Smith was elected governor of New York in 1918 and quickly earned national recognition for the honesty and efficiency of his administration.

Known to his admirers as the Common Man, Al Smith embodied a style of urban democracy often championed by American Catholics, who were not fully aware of just how "foreign" they seemed to citizens of rural and small-town America. It was therefore quite a shock for Smith to encounter the hostility that marked his forays into national politics. His first came in 1924, when he unsuccessfully sought the Democratic Presidential nomination, the second in 1928, when he won the nomination and faced the Republican candidate, Herbert Hoover, in the general election. The Ku Klux Klan—a white supremacist organization founded in 1866 in Pulaski, Tennessee, to terrorize freed slaves in the South—had been revived in 1915 and now focused its hatred on Catholics and Jews as well as African Americans. Anti-Catholicism appealed to many respectable citizens as well. The Oregon state legislature, for example, ruled in 1922 that all children in the state must attend public schools. Although the law was overturned by the U.S. Supreme Court in 1925, it was symptomatic of a widespread fear of foreigners and immigrants in the 1920s, an anxiety that spurred renewed charges that Catholicism was an "alien" faith.

In the early days of the 1928 Presidential campaign, some Protestant churches in Georgia displayed a photograph of Smith at the dedication of the Holland Tunnel linking New Jersey and New York. A caption claimed that it was a tunnel to Rome designed to give the pope easy access to Smith once he inhabited the White House. More disturbing was "An Open Letter to the Honorable Alfred E. Smith" from Charles Marshall, a distinguished New York attorney, which appeared in the *Atlantic Monthly* of April 1927, before Smith had announced his candidacy. Marshall

This political cartoon from 1928 depicts the bigotry displayed against Al Smith during his Presidential campaign. Smith opposed Prohibition, which his enemies used as an issue to hide their "Religious Prejudice," written on the sniper's arm.

alleged that Smith, as a Catholic, was required to demand special privileges for his own church at the expense of all others.

Although Marshall misinterpreted the teachings of the church, his pointed question to Smith ("whether, as a Roman Catholic, you accept as authoritative the teaching of the Roman Catholic Church") put the candidate in an awkward position. As Smith wrote in his autobiography, "The Marshall letter raised questions of theology. . . . At no time in my life have I ever pretended any fundamental knowledge of the subject."

None of the Presidential candidates who preceded Al Smith—Protestants all—had ever been obliged to comment on technical matters of church doctrine. Smith initially told an advisor that he would not dignify Marshall's charges: "I have been a Catholic all my life . . . and I never heard of these encyclicals and papal bulls" that Marshall had cited in his letter. With the help of Father Francis P. Duffy, a theologian better known as the chaplain of the Fighting 69th, the celebrated New York regiment that had fought valiantly in World War I, Smith finally crafted a reply to Marshall: "I believe in the worship of God according to the faith and practice of the Roman Catholic Church," he wrote in the *Atlantic Monthly*. "I recognize no power in the institutions of my Church to interfere with the operations of the Constitution of the United States or the enforcement of the law of the land. . . . I believe in the absolute separation of Church and State and in the strict enforcement of the provisions of the Constitution that Congress shall make no law respecting an establishment of religion or prohibiting the free exercise thereof." Then he concluded, "In this spirit, I join with fellow Americans of all creeds in a fervent prayer that never again in this land will any public servant be challenged because of the faith in which he has tried to walk humbly with his God."

Charles Marshall replied that "Governor Smith, even plus the Reverend Father Duffy, is not the Church," by which he meant that they did not speak for the entire church, which was precisely their point. Father Duffy hastily informed Marshall through an intermediary "that there can be in the Catholic Church various schools of thought. He [Marshall] cannot deny that the hierarchy of America is opposed to union of Church and State. . . . We are Catholics and we are Americans, and to both loyalties we stick." Father Duffy's belief in pluralism—the recognition of more than one point of view as legitimate—and his understanding that church doctrine had developed over time, were shared by numerous influential Catholic thinkers. In acknowledging that "it was a matter of keen joy to me to take advantage of Governor Smith's prestige to win a victory over the opposing Catholic school of thought," Duffy clearly conceded that some in the church disagreed with his position.

For Al Smith, there would be no victory over Herbert Hoover, who won the Presidency by a margin of 444 electoral votes to 87 for Smith. At a time of widespread if fragile prosperity (rampant speculation in the stock market would lead to a market crash in 1929; a worldwide depression was underway by 1930), the Republican was a strong candidate who sported an impressive résumé. Although anti-Catholicism and Smith's opposition to Prohibition (which had outlawed the sale and distribution of alcoholic beverages) contributed to his defeat, his campaign shored up the urban foundation of the Democratic party and paved the way for electoral victories yet to come.

In 1933 Al Smith wrote a laudatory preface for a biography of Father Charles Coughlin, the star of a weekly radio program broadcast nationally. Smith wrote that Coughlin "has righteousness in his heart and brilliance in his mind." Smith came to regret praising a man he later dismissed as a "crackpot," but in the early 1930s Father Coughlin was clearly among the most popular and admired men in the United States. Charles Coughlin was born in Hamilton, Ontario, in 1891, to an Irish-American father and a Canadian mother. Encouraged by his mother to pursue a

Father Charles E. Coughlin, the "radio priest" with the rousing speaking style, began the 1930s as one of the most popular figures in the nation and ended the decade as one of the most controversial because of his bitter attacks against President Roosevelt and others.

priestly vocation, Coughlin was ordained in 1916. He taught briefly in Canada before moving to Detroit in 1923; three years later he was assigned to a new parish in suburban Royal Oak, Michigan. Two weeks after the Shrine of the Little Flower Church was completed in 1926 (it was dedicated to St. Therese of Lisieux, a French nun known as the Little Flower), the Ku Klux Klan burned a cross on the church's lawn.

Coughlin persuaded the manager of radio station WJR in Detroit to make airtime available for the priest to dramatize the plight of his besieged parish. Commercial radio was barely five years old and there had been no regularly scheduled Catholic programming before, but Coughlin's powerful voice and blunt message quickly won him a large listening audience. He organized the Radio League of the Little Flower, whose members not only sustained his radio broadcasts but also financed a massive new Shrine of the Little Flower in Royal Oak.

Coughlin's radio addresses were initially confined to religious themes, but with the onset of the Great Depression in 1930 he shifted his focus to topics of economic and political significance. Beginning in the fall of that year his broadcasts were carried nationwide over the Columbia Broadcasting System. When the network canceled his controversial program a year later Coughlin simply shifted his broadcasts to a network of independent stations. The program drew as many as a million listeners per week, making Coughlin perhaps the most popular radio performer in 1930s America.

Like Father John A. Ryan, Charles Coughlin was deeply influenced by both the tradition of midwestern populism and the social encyclicals of popes Leo XIII and Pius XI, who updated Leo's 1891 *Rerum Novarum* with the encyclical *Quadragesimo Anno* (a letter marking the 40th anniversary of modern Catholic social thought). Coughlin, however, was much more flamboyant than Ryan and was all too willing to resort to personal attacks. In a 1932 broadcast, for example, he called President Herbert Hoover "the banker's friend, the Holy Ghost of the rich, the protective angel of Wall Street." Some church authorities grew concerned with Coughlin's growing notoriety but feared a backlash should they speak out against him. Coughlin strongly supported the election of Franklin D. Roosevelt to the Presidency in 1932 ("It is Roosevelt or ruin," he bellowed in a broadcast aired during the campaign), but was bitterly disappointed to discover that Roosevelt planned to ignore him once he was in office.

In the early stages of his radio career, Coughlin appealed to listeners from a wide variety of religious and ethnic backgrounds. After his rejection by the President, however, Coughlin became a bitter critic of Roosevelt's strategies to combat the depression, and in 1937 he began to lash out at Anglo-American and Jewish financiers, employing ugly stereotypes against the latter. When his own bishop in Detroit failed to silence him, Cardinal George Mundelein of Chicago declared in 1938, "Father Coughlin has the right to express his views on current events, but he is not authorized to speak for the Catholic Church, nor does he represent the doctrine or sentiments of the Church." Coughlin's attempt to create a third political party ended in dismal failure; in 1940 his radio broadcasts ceased and he retreated into obscurity.

Coughlin's bitterness toward Franklin D. Roosevelt was not shared by a substantial majority of American Catholics. Amid the economic hardships endured by millions during the depression, the 1930s saw an unprecedented number of Catholics elevated to positions of prominence in the executive and judicial branches of the federal government. One of Roosevelt's most trusted advisors was James A. Farley, an Irish American from New York whose appointment as Postmaster General of the United States obscured his more significant contribution as one of the architects of the New Deal coalition that established the Democrats as America's majority party for decades to come. In 1933 the President appointed Michigan attorney Frank Murphy to serve as governor general of the Philippines. His Catholicism was deeply appreciated by the Filipino people, many of whom had long believed that America was a strictly Protestant society. Then, after serving a term as governor of Michigan, Murphy was named Attorney General of the United States in 1939. A year later, President Roosevelt appointed him to the U.S. Supreme Court.

Frank Murphy often quoted the church's social encyclicals when outlining his own political philosophy. In a 1933 article for *Commonweal,* a journal of Catholic opinion founded in 1924 by a layman, Michael Williams, Murphy wrote: "Forty-two years ago the great Pontiff, Leo XIII, pointed the way in his encyclical, 'On the Condition of the Working Classes.' He said: 'Rulers should . . . anxiously safeguard the community and all its members.' " Catholics applauded when President Roosevelt praised the encyclical *Quadragesimo Anno* as "one of the greatest documents of modern times." John A. Ryan, who was dubbed the Right Reverend New Dealer, came to the aid of the President on a 1936 radio broadcast sponsored by the Democratic National Committee. In it Ryan condemned Roosevelt's enemy, Father Charles Coughlin, and described the New Deal's programs of economic recovery as "mild installments of too long delayed social justice," a possible reference to the bold programs Ryan had proposed for the Bishops' Program nearly two decades earlier.

One American Catholic rose to prominence in the 1930s by insisting that the New Deal's programs were in fact far too mild, because they did not address the spiritual dimensions of human suffering and poverty. Dorothy Day, who founded the Catholic Worker movement in 1933 was

Catholic politician James A. Farley addresses the 1940 Democratic National Convention in Chicago. Farley's name was placed in nomination at the convention after he resigned his position as Postmaster General of the United States in protest of Franklin D. Roosevelt's decision to seek an unprecedented third term as President.

born in Brooklyn, New York, in 1897 but grew up in San Francisco and Chicago, the daughter of a sportswriter and a housewife who both came from southern Protestant backgrounds but were indifferent to organized religion. Day later blamed her family's lack of warmth on their "Anglo Saxon" ancestry. "We could never be free with others, never put our arms around them companionably as I have seen Italian boys doing," she wrote in her autobiography, *The Long Loneliness* (1952). She was drawn to the urban, immigrant world of Catholic America, but the church itself remained alien and forbidding to Dorothy in her adolescence and young adulthood.

Following two years at the University of Illinois, Dorothy Day moved with her family in 1916 to New York City, where the aspiring young journalist quickly gravitated to the bohemian scene of Greenwich Village. A self-proclaimed "rebel girl," she wrote for a socialist newspaper and experienced brief romantic flings with the playwright Eugene O'Neill and the radical journalist Mike Gold. In 1925 Day entered into a common-law marriage with an anarchist(an advocate of the complete absence of government) and fisherman named Forster Batterham; the couple lived in a beach house in a secluded area of Staten Island, New York. When their daughter Tamar was born, Day immediately decided to have the infant baptized into the Catholic Church. "I knew I was not going to have her floundering through many years as I had done," she wrote in *The Long Loneliness*. Day then decided to join the church herself, which brought her relationship with Batterham to an end.

Over the next several years Day traveled with Tamar to Mexico and California before returning to New York, where she occasionally wrote for *Commonweal* and other Catholic magazines while searching for a way to serve the church more fully. During a 1932 visit to the National Shrine of the Immaculate Conception in Washington, D.C., Day recounted in her autobiography, she realized that few Catholics in the working class were aware of the church's teachings on social issues. "So I offered up my prayers that morning that some way be shown me to do the work that I wanted to do for labor."

"It has long been my contention that Dorothy Day is a saint—not a 'gingerbread' saint or a 'holy card' saint, but a modern day devoted daughter of the Church, a daughter who shunned personal aggrandizement and wished that her work, and the work of those who labored at her side on behalf of the poor, might be the hallmark of her life rather than her own self."
—Cardinal John O'Connor

The Inaugural Issue of the Catholic Worker

The Catholic Worker is a monthly newspaper founded by Dorothy Day and Peter Maurin. The paper has sold for a penny per copy since its origins in May 1933, at the height of the Great Depression. In the first issue of the Catholic Worker, *Dorothy Day set the tone for the paper's simple yet powerful and enduring message.*

To Our Readers

For those who are sitting on park benches in the warm spring sunlight.

For those who are huddling in shelters trying to escape the rain.

For those who are walking the streets in the all but futile search for work.

For those who think that there is no hope for the future, no recognition of their plight, this little paper is addressed.

It is printed to call their attention to the fact that the Catholic Church has a social program—to let them know that there are men of God who are working not only for their spiritual, but for their material welfare.

Filling A Need

It's time there was a Catholic paper printed for the unemployed. The fundamental aim of most radical sheets is the conversion of its readers to Radicalism and Atheism.

Is it not possible to be radical and not atheist?

Is it not possible to protest, to expose, to complain, to point out abuses and demand reforms without desiring the overthrow of religion?

In an attempt to popularize and make known the encyclicals of the popes in regard to social justice and the program put forth by the church for the 'reconstruction of the social order,' this news sheet, THE CATHOLIC WORKER, is started.

It is not as yet known whether it will be a monthly, a fortnightly, or a weekly. It all depends on the funds collected for the printing and distribution. Those who can subscribe, and those who can donate, are asked to do so.

This first number of THE CATHOLIC WORKER was planned, written and edited in the kitchen of a tenement on Fifteenth Street, on subway platforms, on the "L", the ferry. There is no editorial office, no overhead in the way of telephone or electricity; no salaries paid.

The money for the printing of the first issue was raised by begging small contributions from friends. A colored priest in Newark sent us ten dollars and the prayers of his congregation. A colored sister in New Jersey, garbed also in holy poverty, sent us a dollar. The rest of it the editors squeezed out of their own earnings, and at that they were using money necessary to pay milk bills, gas bills, electric light bills.

By accepting delay the utilities did not know that they were furthering the cause of social justice. They were, for the time being, unwitting cooperators.

We are asking our friends and sympathizers to help out towards the next issue by sending contributions to THE CATHOLIC WORKER, which will be edited this month at 54 Scarboro Avenue, Rosebank, Staten Island.

Next month someone may donate us an office. Who knows?

It is cheering to remember that Jesus Christ wandered this earth with no place to lay His Head. *The foxes have holes and the birds of the air their nests, but the Son of Man has no place to lay His Head.* And when we consider our fly-by-night existence, our uncertainty, we remember (with pride at sharing the honor), that the disciples supped by the seashore and wandered through corn fields picking the ears from the stalks wherewith to make their frugal meals.

Shortly after Day returned to New York a disheveled Frenchman named Peter Maurin appeared in the doorway of her apartment. He had been sent to meet Day by George Shuster, a *Commonweal* editor who, aware of her radical background, decided, as he wrote in a 1974 memoir, that "Dorothy was the only person to whom I could have sent Peter. . . . John A. Ryan would not have known what to do with this strange little man." Shuster meant that Day was unique among American Catholics for the depth of her radicalism and the breadth of her experience with visionaries such as Peter Maurin, who was dismissed by many as merely eccentric.

Peter Maurin was a wandering philosopher who convinced Dorothy Day to launch a movement devoted to feeding the hungry and sheltering the homeless. The resulting Catholic Worker movement began in Day's New York apartment in early 1933 and quickly spread to many cities in the northeastern and midwestern United States. The movement's appeal lay partly in the directness of its approach: Catholic Workers believed that Jesus was to be found in the poor and suffering (whom they called ambassadors of Christ) and that it was the responsibility of Christians to perform works of mercy rather than wait for agencies of the state or church to act. Each Catholic Worker community centered around a "house of hospitality" where "workers" (the poor) and "scholars" (movement volunteers) shared their talents as well as their needs. Many observers mistakenly believed the Catholic Worker movement to be a labor organization, but Peter Maurin and Dorothy Day strongly condemned both the American industrial system and the class-conscious strategies of union leaders. "Strikes don't strike me," Maurin wrote in one of his "Easy Essays," short meditations published in the monthly *Catholic Worker* newspaper. He urged all Catholics to abandon the cities and return to the land, where they could live in simple yet spiritually rich harmony.

Day and Maurin described themselves as Catholic anarchists, because they denied the legitimacy of the state: Day urged Catholic Workers not to vote, and her movement and newspaper refused to file for tax-exempt charitable status. She rejected the New Deal's social welfare programs as

un-Christian, because they enslaved the poor in a dependent relationship with the federal government. She advocated a philosophy known as personalism, the belief that every human being is endowed by God with dignity, grace, and purpose. The goal of all genuine communities was to ensure that the "spark of the divine" residing in all women and men could be ignited, enabling them to enter into a more intimate and personal relationship with God their creator. Dorothy Day, along with many Catholic theologians of the 1930s and 1940s, viewed the church as the visible sign of Christ's Mystical Body. In the Mystical Body of Christ, she explained, all people were bound spiritually together so that an injury to one was an injury to all. Each individual was therefore personally responsible for the welfare of others.

Many young people were drawn to the Catholic Worker movement by its charismatic leader, who offered them more meaningful and exciting work in service to the church, in a more dramatic setting than the typical

A meal at St. Anthony's House of Hospitality in Baltimore, about 1940. According to *The Catholic Worker* newspaper, "Houses of hospitality are centers for learning to do the acts of love, so that the poor can receive what is, in justice, theirs, the second coat in our closet, the spare room in our home, a place at our table. Anything beyond what we immediately need belongs to those who go without."

parish could provide. One young Catholic Worker recalled attending a lecture by Day in 1934 at John Carroll University, a Jesuit institution in Cleveland, Ohio: "The next day, down in the cafeteria . . . she was being discussed at great length. . . . They were talking about how beautiful she was. She talked the entire lecture with a cigarette hanging out of a corner of her mouth, with a beret on." A priest active in the 1930s labor movement testified that "she was the inspiration for everything I did. She was the most natural, relaxed, humble, self-sacrificing person I ever met."

Dorothy Day was also a very gifted writer and editor who used her *Catholic Worker* newspaper to introduce American Catholics to exciting developments taking place in the church around the world, especially in Europe, which saw a major revival of Catholic literary and intellectual life in the 1920s and 1930s. In recognition of the increasing desire of the laity to express their faith in the public arena, Pope Pius XI launched the Catholic Action movement in 1922. The pope defined Catholic Action as "the participation of the laity in the apostolate [works inspired by the example of Christ's apostles] of the hierarchy." In Europe, Catholic Action sponsored such well-organized groups as the Young Christian Workers (YCW) and the Young Christian Students (YCS), whose members sought to expose their peers to the social teachings of the church.

In the United States the Catholic Action philosophy was reflected not only in chapters of the YCW and YCS but also in dozens of organizations that sprang up catering to virtually every interest and occupation. There were groups for Catholics lawyers, doctors, and philosophers; a Catholic Book Club and a Catholic Poetry Society; an Association of Catholic Trade Unionists and a Catholic Labor Defense League. Although it was not unusual for religious denominations to sponsor special-interest groups, the proliferation of such Catholic societies in the 1930s indicated the desire of church leaders to provide a wholly separate cultural as well as spiritual life to lay people.

Although the Catholic Worker movement was viewed as controversial by many in the church, it fit neatly into an emerging network of "lay apostolates," programs linked to the Catholic Action network but often

The Boy Scout troop of St. Peter Claver's Catholic Church of Philadelphia poses in 1936. In the 1920s and 1930s a multitude of Catholic organizations emerged to serve the social and spiritual needs of the church community in all parts of the nation.

directed by lay members. The Catholic Worker movement reflected its founder's appreciation of the American tradition of voluntary social activism conducted at the grassroots level. Dorothy Day made an enduring contribution to American Catholic life, not only by offering an example of service to the poor but by showing how the faith could be integrated into every aspect of one's life. In a tribute published in *Commonweal* after her death in 1980, author David J. O'Brien called Dorothy Day "the most significant, interesting, and influential person in the history of American Catholicism."

When the United States entered World War II in 1941, however, Day's insistence that true Christians must also be pacifists alienated her from many members of the Catholic Worker movement. The movement survived, but it would undergo dramatic changes, along with virtually all other American institutions touched by the war.

Chapter 6

The Uneasy Triumph of Catholic America

World War II dramatically reshaped American life. While millions of Americans served in the armed forces, even more contributed on the home front by working in war industries or taking on jobs once performed by those now serving in the military. Vast numbers of Americans moved from regions of the country where their families had lived for generations to strange new cities. When the United States emerged victorious from war in 1945, many citizens wondered if the changes of wartime were permanent or if a more traditional way of life could be restored.

A widespread postwar housing crisis served notice that more changes were coming. American Catholics were especially hard hit by shortages of decent housing, because they were so heavily concentrated in urban areas, where very little new housing was built during the years of the Depression and war. Mass-produced suburban homes did not become an option for many until the early 1950s. A few Catholics sought to create their own communities in the immediate postwar period. A group from the Bronx, New York, attempted to live as lay apostles (women and men devoted to living out the church's teachings without formally entering religious life) on a communally owned parcel of land near West Nyack, New York, named Marycrest in honor of the Blessed Virgin Mary. Dorothy and Ed Willock were the most zealous couple at Marycrest. He was the editor of *Integrity,* a radical Catholic magazine inspired by the example of the Catholic Worker movement.

The Willocks hoped to foster a new spirituality of the family at Marycrest, a place where large families could be celebrated as a sign of God's abundant providence. The Willocks had 12 children, a number only slightly above average among Marycresters, who built homes for each other's families on weekends while they worked in New York City during the week. Marycresters were committed to simple living and voluntary poverty; the original families shared a conviction that American consumer values were incompatible with a genuinely Christian lifestyle. The sacrifices demanded at Marycrest proved too severe for more than a few devoted families to endure, but they inspired other Catholics who remained in the city to pursue their own versions of the family apostolate.

A number of young Catholic women of the late 1940s and 1950s were attracted to the lay spirituality fostered at the Grail community near Loveland, Ohio. The Grail originated in the Netherlands as the Society of the Women of Nazareth. In 1940 two Dutch women, Lydwine van Kersbergen and Joan Overboss, brought the movement (now known as the Grail, a name reflecting the romantic nature of the movement's spiritual quest) to the United States. Their avowed aim was to "counteract in the world all masculine hardness, all the angles of the masculine character, all cruelty, all the results of alcohol and prostitution and sin and capitalism, which are ultramasculine, and to Christianize that with a womanly charity." Grailville, the movement's rural headquarters, was dubbed "the Mystical Body [of Christ] in miniature," because it offered courses and retreats for women from across the country interested in exploring the relationship between personal spirituality and lay activism in the church. By the 1950s the Grail had 600 active members, both married and single, as well as 100 lifetime members who were committed to celibacy, complete abstinence from sex. Several thousand additional women took part in Grail-sponsored programs in many parts of the United States, helping to organize credit unions, for example, in impoverished sections of Detroit, Cincinnati, and Brooklyn, New York. The Grail also sent teams of women to developing nations, where they worked on self-help programs similar to those created by the Peace Corps in the early 1960s.

Despite the attractions of rural religious communities and the dramatic growth of suburbia in the years following World War II, the great majority of American Catholics continued to reside in densely populated urban centers well into the 1950s. Their deep loyalty to ethnic parish neighborhoods often provoked resistance to change. During the war, hundreds of thousands of African Americans had emigrated from the South to northern cities in pursuit of work. In Detroit, which saw an influx of 60,000 African Americans between 1940 and 1946, Polish-American Catholics resisted the construction of new federally funded housing on the city's North Side, fearing that the stability of their nearby parishes would be threatened by African-American outsiders. Riots broke out in February 1942 when the first African-American families attempted to move into the project, the Sojourner Truth Homes, named after an African-American abolitionist who in the 1840s and 1850s worked with white reformers in the American Anti-Slavery Society.

The blatant racism of America's enemies in World War II inspired increasing calls for social harmony on the home front. Speaking to a gathering of 30,000 at a 1945 rally, New York's archbishop, Cardinal Francis Spellman, declared that "a real American" was one who fought "the spread of bigotry." Yet that same year the noted anthropologist Margaret Mead, in an essay on "How Religion Has Fared in the Melting Pot," criticized "an immigrant community which is both foreign and Catholic." Mead accused the church of trying to "keep its young people separate from the community" and "isolating them from the mainstream of American life."

Women at the Ohio Grailville community in the 1950s baked bread for themselves and for sale to the local community. The wall behind them reads, "He fed them with the fat of wheat."

Margaret Mead was not a Catholic, but her charges echoed concerns arising from within the church as well. A Jesuit priest, John LaFarge, was the leading exponent of the "interracial apostolate," a Catholic Action program that emphasized the unity of all human beings within the Mystical Body of Christ. In February 1944 a Jesuit at Saint Louis University preached a sermon denouncing racial segregation as a sin; the entire congregation rose as one after he urged them to pledge their commitment to racial justice. Later that year that same university became the first institution of higher learning in a former slave state to admit African-American students. Amid the ensuing controversy, however, the Jesuits most fervently involved in the interracial apostolate were reassigned to other parts of the country.

The Catholic campaign against racial segregation exposed a rift in the church that mirrored divisions in the broader society. Although the church clearly condemned segregation, many urban pastors and their congregations wished to preserve the ethnicity of parishes that had sustained immigrant families for decades. American Protestant and Jewish leaders were often at the forefront of the battle against racism, but their congregations were generally free to move their places of worship out of older, inner-city neighborhoods. Catholic parishes could not simply move, because they were administered not by the congregation itself but by diocesan authorities. Urban Catholics often viewed the parish as sacred space; one Chicago pastor even referred to his parish as "Our Lady of the Boulevard."

Father John LaFarge came from a wealthy, sophisticated background. Like many Catholics in the interracial movement, he was dismayed by the "tribalism" of urban Catholic communities. "Unfortunately there is very painful evidence about the Polish clergy," LaFarge wrote to the Catholic social reformer John A. Ryan in 1943 in response to the incidents in Detroit. "I have not heard about Italian clergy, but knowing how some of the foreign clergy behave in these neighborhood questions I should be by no means surprised if some of them took an equally unjustified attitude."

A Jesuit priest from a prominent Rhode Island family, John LaFarge fought for the civil rights of African Americans. In one of his last public acts, he participated in the August 1963 March on Washington and witnessed the Rev. Martin Luther King, Jr.'s, "I Have a Dream" speech.

The first communion class of Our Lady of Perpetual Help Church in Baltimore, 1955. Some African-American Catholics in the 1940s and '50s preferred separate parishes, while others sought integration into parishes dominated by members of white ethnic groups.

LaFarge also believed that the small community of African-American Catholics (between 2 and 3 percent of the total black population) should shed its own racial identity in the name of Christian unity within the Mystical Body of Christ. This view typified the Catholic Action approach so prevalent among activists of the 1930s and 1940s, but it conflicted with the aspirations of many African-American Catholics to preserve their own ethnic identity. LaFarge had a troubled relationship with Thomas Wyatt Turner, who founded the Federated Colored Catholics in 1925. This organization of laypersons declared that its "sole purpose" was "to weld all others [African-American Catholics] into a solid unit for race betterment." LaFarge had informed Turner in 1932 that the church's leadership had the "right and the duty" to advise black Catholics on the proper strategies for achieving racial equality in both church and society.

In the 1940s the war against racist, fascist powers in Europe and Asia undermined racial segregation on the home front, but this caused a dilemma for African-American Catholics who felt they should have their own parishes, like the members of other ethnic groups. In 1945 Boston's Cardinal Richard Cushing agreed to found an African-American parish, "as the Italians, French, Syrians, and other groups have for theirs within the city." Cardinal Cushing carefully noted, however, that "this new church is not established in accordance with any concept of 'segregation.' " An African-American newspaper still strongly objected that the Catholic Church was "extending segregation" at a time when "the colored people of Boston have won several fights against Jim Crow [a term that originally referred to segregation laws in the South but later signified all forms of discrimination against African Americans] clubs and places of entertainment." In 1945 the Chicago council of the Federated Colored Catholics proclaimed that "the effectiveness of its program lies in its affiliation with Catholics of all races." The desire for racial integration was a primary theme of the post-war civil rights movement, but African-American Catholics did not always feel free to assert their own interests in the absense of black leadership within the church.

In the late 1940s and 1950s the leaders of the Catholic interracial movement often stressed the importance of protecting African Americans from appeals made by communists. Anticommunism was the dominant political issue in American Catholic life between 1945 and 1960, as it was indeed in American life generally. Anticommunism was especially important to Catholics, however, because it offered a vehicle for blending patriotic and religious concerns in a manner that would finally put to rest nativist suspicions concerning their legitimacy as full-fledged Americans.

Unlike many Americans who grew concerned with communism only after the Soviet Union erected an "iron curtain" (a term coined by British statesman Winston Churchill to portray the ruthlessness of Soviet power) around Eastern Europe shortly after the end of World War II, Catholics had been deeply hostile to communism since the 1920s, when the U.S.S.R. began persecuting Christians. After the Spanish Civil War broke out in 1936, most American Catholics supported the forces of General Francisco Franco, who sought to oust the Soviet-backed regime that had replaced the Spanish monarchy in 1931. Franco was backed by the Spanish church as well as by the fascist governments of Germany and Italy, prompting many American liberals to link Catholic support of Franco with sympathy for the dictators Adolf Hitler and Benito Mussolini. In response, Fulton J. Sheen, a theologian and a popular radio commentator,

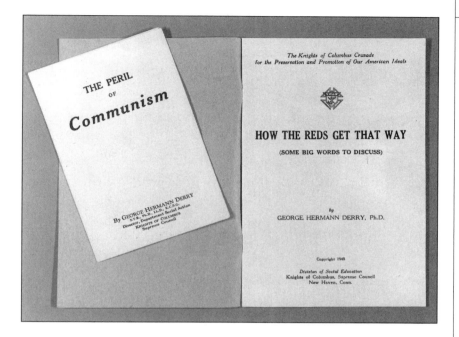

The Knights of Columbus Crusade
for the Preservation and Promotion of Our American Ideals

HOW THE REDS GET THAT WAY

(SOME BIG WORDS TO DISCUSS)

by
GEORGE HERMANN DERRY, Ph.D.

Copyright 1948

Division of Social Education
Knights of Columbus, Supreme Council
New Haven, Conn.

THE PERIL OF Communism

By GEORGE HERMANN DERRY
S.T.B., Ph.D., LL.D., K.C.S.G.
Director, Department Social Action
KNIGHTS OF COLUMBUS
Supreme Council

In the late 1940s the Division of Social Education of the Knights of Columbus issued pamphlets in support of the group's Crusade for the Preservation and Promotion of American Ideals. Many Catholic organizations sponsored anticommunist activities during the cold war era.

argued in 1937 that there was "no essential difference" between fascism and communism; the church opposed both.

While Catholics were wary of America's World War II alliance with the Soviet Union, all but a small number recognized the necessity of defeating the Axis powers (Germany, Italy, and Japan). As soon as the Soviets occupied the nations of Eastern Europe, however, Catholics renewed their attacks on communism, which many viewed as not only evil but demonically inspired (on his popular radio program, "The Catholic Hour," Fulton J. Sheen referred to the Soviet Union as "the Mystical Body of Satan"). Father John F. Cronin, a Baltimore seminary professor, was one of the most knowledgeable and trusted students of the communist threat at home and abroad in the postwar years. He was a key advisor to a young California congressman, Richard M. Nixon, whose investigations of an alleged former communist, Alger Hiss, dominated the nation's headlines in 1949. The public response to the Hiss case paved the way for the rise of the most notorious Catholic anticommunist of the cold war years, Joseph R. McCarthy, the junior senator from Wisconsin.

Between 1950 and 1954 Joe McCarthy dominated American political life with his senate investigations of alleged communist infiltration of the federal government. He made dozens of reckless accusations that almost always proved groundless, but his popularity reflected a widespread, and not wholly inaccurate view, that communism had in fact exerted a significant, if secretive, influence in parts of the American labor movement as well as the entertainment industry since the 1930s. Although McCarthy may, as some of his critics alleged, have initially been urged to focus on the communism issue by a Jesuit from Georgetown University, Edmund Walsh, the senator was above all a political opportunist who showed little concern for the religious aspects of his crusade. He was, however, championed by many American Catholic newspapers and magazines (though *Commonweal* and *America*, two of the most prominent publications, were highly critical of McCarthy's tactics) and received thunderous ovations when he appeared at such gatherings as a Chicago St. Patrick's Day dinner or a 1954 breakfast meeting of 6,000 Catholic policemen in New York City. McCarthy disgraced himself that same year during televised hearings investigating alleged communist infiltration of the U.S. Army, then faded quickly into oblivion.

Nineteen fifty-four also witnessed the emergence of a Catholic leader in South Vietnam, a nation created when the former French colony of Vietnam was divided into two parts. The communist Viet Minh, who had driven the French from Vietnam in the climactic battle of Dien Bien Phu in the spring of 1954, assumed control of the North, while the American-backed government of Ngo Dinh Diem took charge in South Vietnam. Diem had spent time in Catholic seminaries in New York and New Jersey during a period of exile in the early 1950s, when he made numerous important contacts with U.S. political and religious leaders. After he became South Vietnam's prime minister Diem was fervently supported by the leader of the American hierarchy, Cardinal Francis Spellman, and his leadership was highly praised in a best-selling book of 1956, *Deliver Us from Evil*, by a young American Catholic from St. Louis, Thomas A. Dooley. As a naval medical officer Dooley had aided in the massive refugee campaign of 1954–55, which saw nearly a million Vietnamese

Catholics moved from the communist north to South Vietnam.

In *Deliver Us from Evil* Dooley described the Catholic refugees as pilgrims seeking religious freedom, an image that quickly took hold in the American imagination and further enhanced the stature of Catholicism at home and abroad. In Vietnam, Dooley wrote, "I had watched tough U.S. sailors become tender nurses for sick babies and dying old men. I had seen inhuman torture and suffering elevate weak men to lofty heights of spiritual nobility. I knew now why organized godlessness can never kill the divine spark that burns within even the humblest human."

Catholic political figures such as Senator Mike Mansfield of Montana and Senator John F. Kennedy of Massachusetts were among the most enthusiastic supporters of the Diem regime. The Vietnamese leader was often compared to George Washington, with his refugee constituents being likened to the pilgrims who had come to America in search of religious freedom and opportunity. Although Diem's ardent Catholicism was downplayed by his supporters to avoid arousing suspicions of Vatican influence over his administration, Diem's popularity in America suggested that Catholics might have an important role in shaping this nation's foreign policy.

A highly distinctive aspect of Catholic anticommunism in the 1950s was found in believers' deep devotion to the Blessed Virgin Mary, whose purity, simplicity, and humility were sharply contrasted with the ruthlessly atheistic, militaristic character of Soviet communism. Mary had always been a central figure in the devotional Catholicism of the immigrant church, but her role grew even greater when, in 1950, Pope Pius XII promulgated the Assumption, the teaching that "the Immaculate Mother of God, Mary ever Virgin, when the course of her earthly life was finished, was taken up body and soul into the glory of heaven." Private devotions to Mary were a central feature of Catholic life in Europe as well as America,

Francis Spellman grew up in Massachusetts but rose to become Cardinal Archbishop of New York. From the late 1930s until his death in 1967 he was the most powerful member of the American church hierarchy, called by some the "American Pope."

especially between the mid 19th and mid 20th centuries. By the 1950s virtually every parish in America held a May procession in honor of Mary, culminating with the crowning of a statue of Mary by a student specially chosen for the honor. As more Catholics moved from urban ethnic neighborhoods to suburbia, Marian devotions grew more widespread and assumed a more public character as a central feature of Catholic anti-communism.

In 1946 a Catholic layman, John Haffert, created the Blue Army of Fatima, a group devoted to promoting an apparition of the Blessed Mother claimed by three Portuguese children in 1917 that inspired millions of Catholics worldwide. One of the Fatima eyewitnesses later reported that during the vision Mary had instructed Catholics to perform certain devotions that would result in the conversion of the Soviet Union to Catholicism (the Blue Army noted that the vision at Fatima occurred just as the Russian Revolution was beginning). During the cold war years, Marian apparitions were reported at a number of sites, including on a farm in Necedah, Wisconsin, where reports of the Blessed Mother's appearance to Mary Ann Van Hoof attracted nearly 100,000 pilgrims in the summer of 1950. The consoling image of Mary enabled millions of

Members of the Poor Handmaids of Jesus Christ, a women's religious community, participate in a May procession in honor of the Blessed Virgin Mary.

The Trappist monk Thomas Merton, center, with a group of students ("scholastics") at the Abbey of Gethsemani near Bardstown, Kentucky. In 1965 Merton was freed from his ordinary duties and moved into a cinderblock "hermitage" on the grounds of the monastery.

American Catholics to feel that they were under the protection of the Blessed Mother and her Son, Jesus Christ, at times of great peril.

The special devotion to Mary practiced by American Catholics in the 1950s did not prevent numerous observers from declaring that the people of that church had earned unprecedented acceptance within the broader society. In a highly influential book, *Protestant-Catholic-Jew* (1955), the social critic Will Herberg explained that America could no longer properly be described as a Protestant country, because Catholics and Jews had been fully blended into the national mainstream. In surrendering the ethnic distinctiveness that marked the century (1845–1945) of the immigrant church, Herberg argued, Catholics had developed an even stronger allegiance to the church, which both ministered to their spiritual needs and provided a strong sense of communal identity as a substitute for ethnic commitments. "The three great religious communions—Protestant, Catholic, and Jewish—constitute the three great American religions, the 'religions of democracy,' " wrote Herberg. "The Catholic attitude," he concluded, "is increasingly that of a substantial minority [group] with a strong sense of self-assurance."

The prestige and popularity enjoyed by many Catholic Americans in the decade following World War II certainly seemed to confirm Herberg's thesis. One of the most successful books of the late 1940s was Thomas Merton's memoir, *The Seven Storey Mountain* (1948), his story as a young man who had forsaken a life of sensual and intellectual pleasures for the simple yet demanding life of a monk at a Kentucky monastery. Merton's account of his prayerful life at the Abbey of Gethsemani appealed to many readers at a time when new atomic weaponry made concerns about the end of the world seem like more than idle speculation. *The Seven Storey Mountain* enjoyed such an impact that Gethsemani and several other monasteries were soon inundated by candidates for monastic life and were forced to construct temporary barracks to respond to this most unexpected postwar housing crisis. In the 1950s Thomas Merton published numerous volumes on the spiritual life, which were avidly read by millions of admirers from a wide variety of religious backgrounds.

In the 1940s and 1950s Hollywood movies offered many positive depictions of Catholic life in America. Bing Crosby portrayed a lovable priest in *Going My Way* (1944) and *The Bells of St. Mary's* (1945), which

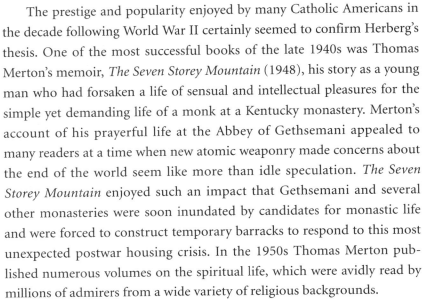

The Bells of St. Mary's was a highly popular 1945 film starring Ingrid Bergman as a nun and Bing Crosby as a priest. The film was one of several from the middle and late 1940s that portrayed Catholicism in a highly favorable light and reflected the optimistic mood of the American church at mid-century.

costarred Ingrid Bergman as a down-to-earth nun. In the much more realistic, Academy Award–winning film *On the Waterfront* (1954), Karl Malden played a tough New Jersey priest who convinces a reluctant former prizefighter, played by Marlon Brando, to help him topple the corrupt leadership of a longshoremen's union. Malden's character was drawn directly from the experience of a Jesuit labor priest, John Corridan, who preached to dock workers that Christ was present on the waterfront, suffered along with them, and called them to seek justice for themselves and their fellows.

The most famous Catholic figure of the 1950s was Fulton J. Sheen, a popular theologian who moved from radio to television in

1952, one year after becoming an auxiliary (assistant) bishop of New York.
For five years Sheen's weekly program,
Life Is Worth Living, was among the
highest-rated shows in the nation.
Though he dressed for the program in
his flowing bishops' cape, Sheen rarely
referred specifically to the teachings of
his church on the program, which featured his own style of highly animated
lectures with the major themes highlighted on an ever-present blackboard.
As a critic for *Time* magazine noted in
1952, Sheen "stressed Christian fundamentals rather than specific Catholic
dogmas." Many of his programs were
not in fact concerned with religion at
all but treated issues shared by viewers
of all backgrounds: the true meaning
of love, the price of ambition, the
value of close family relationships.

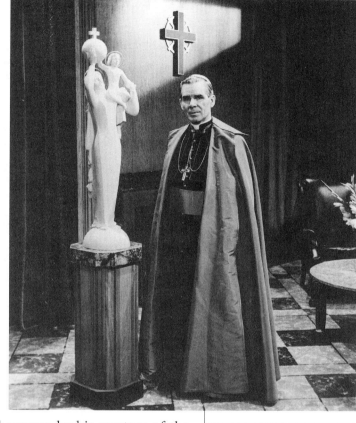

Monsignor Fulton J. Sheen
was the first clergyman to
have a regular television
program. Sheen com-
mented, "Little did I know
. . . that it would be given
to me through radio and
television to address a
greater audience in half
an hour than [Saint] Paul
in all the years of his missionary life."

Sheen's lectures were informed, however, by his mastery of the
Catholic philosophy known as neo-Thomism, based on the thought of St.
Thomas Aquinas, a 13th-century philosopher. The basic theme of
Thomistic thought was that God had endowed human beings with the
capacity to understand, through the use of reason, that the world was created by God and that humans were meant to serve God's purposes in this
world and to be with him in eternity after death. In this philosophy, sin
was understood to be a deliberate act against the natural order created by
God, and upheld by the teachings of the church. Neo-Thomistic thought
encouraged Catholics to believe that God's supernatural grace was
bestowed upon those who followed his commandments and received the
sacraments of the church. Thomism was a complex philosophical system,
but in the gifted hands of Fulton J. Sheen it offered consolation and hope

to those who feared that life was meaningless. In the 1940s and 1950s Sheen was credited with shepherding the conversions to Catholicism of numerous prominent Americans, including Clare Booth Luce, a talented writer who was also the wife of Henry Luce, the founder of the Time-Life magazine publishing empire.

Bishop Sheen's *Life Is Worth Living* program was viewed by 30 million Americans each week, but he was not the only American Catholic to gain great fame in the emerging television industry of the mid 1950s. Ed Sullivan, a former New York entertainment writer, hosted a top-rated Sunday evening variety program. The comedian Jackie Gleason presided over a variety show featuring a weekly skit, *The Honeymooners*, that focused on the trials and tribulations of two childless married couples in Brooklyn, New York. Just as Fulton J. Sheen never discussed Catholic teaching in *Life Is Worth Living*, episodes of *The Honeymooners* made no reference to the Catholic backgrounds of Gleason or his sidekick Art Carney, who portrayed characters with names chosen by Gleason from the New York City phone book for their "all-American" qualities. The neighbors and co-workers of Ralph Kramden and Ed Norton invariably featured Irish and Italian-American surnames, however, and episodes of *The Honeymooners* frequently evoked the close-knit urban, ethnic working-class life of the 1930s and 1940s so familiar to many Catholic viewers.

The Italian-American singer Perry Como also hosted his own highly rated television show in the middle and late 1950s. Sullivan, Gleason, and Como were often lauded in the pages of popular Catholic magazines for their devotion to the church and their charitable works. One of the most glamorous American celebrities of the 1950s, the actress Grace Kelly, was the daughter of Jack Kelly, a self-made Irish-Catholic construction magnate highly prominent in both the Catholic and Democratic party circles of his native Philadelphia. Grace Kelly's engagement and marriage to Prince Rainier of Monaco in 1956 was lavishly covered in the Catholic as well as secular media, often treated as a romantic American fairy tale.

Never before had so many Catholics played such a prominent role in American popular culture. Other than Bishop Sheen, however, these celebrities and entertainers were not primarily concerned with spiritual and theological issues, though they did not shy away from their identity as Catholics. The 1950s also saw the emergence of several Catholic literary artists who drew on their religious imaginations to create some of the most powerful work of the postwar era. Flannery O'Connor grew up in Milledgeville, Georgia, in the 1930s. She developed her skills in the graduate writing program at the University of Iowa in the late 1940s, then lived briefly in Connecticut before returning to her family home, where she lived and wrote until her premature death in 1964.

Flannery O'Connor at a book signing for the release of her novel *Wise Blood* in 1952. Of her vocation as a writer, she said, "The fiction writer represents mystery through manners, grace through nature."

In such stories as "A Good Man Is Hard to Find" and the short novel *Wise Blood*, Flannery O'Connor created memorable, haunted characters who often find themselves in grotesque and violent situations. "I believe," she wrote in a 1955 letter, "and the Church teaches that God is as present in the idiot boy as in the genius." In her stories God's grace is often suddenly bestowed on characters who, though they may be weak, vulnerable, or even deranged, are still "too wise to deny Christ," as she described one such character in a letter to a friend. In a 1957 essay O'Connor explained that the "Catholic sacramental view of life is one that sustains and supports at every turn the vision that the storyteller must have if he is going to write fiction of any depth." Since Catholics believe that sacraments are visible signs of the invisible presence of God, O'Connor's "sacramental view" featured an attentiveness to that presence in many forms. Above all, O'Connor sought to convey something of the mystery of Christian faith: she always wished for some of this mystery to be "left over," as she explained, long after her stories had been read and analyzed.

Flannery O'Connor exerted a great literary and spiritual influence on a small group of friends, including her fellow southern writers Allen Tate, Caroline Gordon, and Walker Percy, each of whom were converts to Catholicism. Jack Kerouac was another Catholic writer of the 1950s who was at the heart of a literary and spiritual community, though the Beat Generation, a term he coined and later regretted, has rarely been viewed as a religious movement. Kerouac grew up in a French-Canadian immigrant neighborhood in Lowell, Massachusetts, in the 1920s and 1930s and did not learn to speak English until enrolling in the local parish grammar school. Like many children of immigrant families, Kerouac relied on his athletic prowess to open doors of opportunity: he won a football scholarship to Columbia University in 1939, but injuries and a growing interest in literature led him in a different direction. In the early 1940s he dropped out of Columbia and began his association with the key figures of the Beat Generation, the young writers Allen Ginsberg, William S. Burroughs, and John Clellon Holmes.

Kerouac told Holmes in 1950 that their generation was "beat" because it had been beaten down by World War II and fears of nuclear annihilation. He was also drawn to the new musical "beat" pioneered by such jazz artists as Charlie Parker and Dizzy Gillespie, whose improvisational "be bop" style was a major inspiration for his writing. Above all, "beat" was for Kerouac an abbreviation of "beatific," a form of blessedness he associated with the beatitudes, pronouncements Jesus made in his Sermon on the Mount, beginning with, "Blessed are the poor in spirit." Kerouac saw writing as a mystical process that brought him into communion with the divine. He told an interviewer in 1958 that his primary desire in life was for "God to show me his face."

Kerouac became notorious in 1957 as the author of *On the Road,* a barely fictionalized account of his restless wanderings across the United States in the company of such boisterous characters as Neal Cassady, a former Denver altar boy and reform-school escapee immortalized in the novel as Dean Moriarty. Much of Kerouac's work, however, took the form of meditations on the Catholic, immigrant neighborhood life he had known in Lowell, a world whose warmth, color, and devotional richness was contrasted with the suburban, consumer-oriented lifestyle that seemed to dominate the 1950s. To critics who saw nothing spiritual about the "beatnik" lifestyle he was wrongly accused of promoting, Kerouac replied simply, "What would Jesus say if I went up to him and said 'May I wear your cross in this world as it is?' " In the late 1950s Kerouac became deeply interested in Buddhism, in part because he felt cut off from the Catholicism of his youth.

Although very few critics noticed the religious dimension in his writing, one American Catholic who confessed to being a Kerouac fan became the First Lady of the United States in 1961. Shortly after her husband, John Fitzgerald Kennedy, was inaugurated as the 35th President, Jacqueline Bouvier Kennedy told reporters that her reading interests ranged from Camus to Kerouac (Albert Camus was a French-Algerian writer popular at the time). John F. Kennedy's election as the nation's first Roman Catholic President was one of the most triumphant events in American Catholic history. Kennedy came from a highly competitive Boston Irish family with roots in the famine emigra-

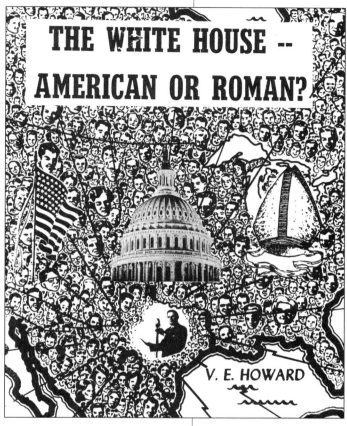

tion of the 1840s. His mother, Rose Fitzgerald Kennedy, was the daughter of John F. ("Honey Fitz") Fitzgerald, a legendary Irish-American politician who served as mayor of Boston on two separate occasions. His father, Joseph P. Kennedy—the son of a saloonkeeper active in Boston Democratic politics—was a highly driven entrepreneur who, after amassing a sizable fortune, was named U.S. Ambassador to the Court of St. James (England) in 1937.

John F. Kennedy, the third of nine children born to Rose and Joseph Kennedy, graduated from Harvard University in 1940. During World War II he commanded a PT (patrol torpedo) boat in the South Pacific; in 1943 the small craft was cut in two by a Japanese destroyer and Kennedy led his men to a nearby island, where they were rescued several days later. In

Many Protestant ministers objected to the Presidential candidacy of John F. Kennedy on religious grounds. This propaganda flyer shows the U.S. government threatened by the influence of the Roman Catholic Church, represented by the pope's mitre.

1946 Kennedy was elected to the U.S. Congress from the 11th congressional district in Massachusetts, in the same waterfront area where his family was already legendary. Despite an undistinguished early political career and the chronic illness that plagued him throughout his adulthood, Kennedy was elected to the U.S. Senate in 1952 after a campaign in which his mother and sisters played a highly visible role. In 1956 he nearly captured the Democratic party's vice-presidential nomination; his charismatic performance at the party's convention that year marked him as a rising star and a likely contender for the Presidency in 1960.

Kennedy and his closest advisers—including his father, who helped bankroll his son's campaigns—were fully aware that his Catholicism represented the greatest obstacle to victory in 1960. In a March 1959 interview with *Look* magazine Kennedy sought to defuse the religion issue before it had a chance to disrupt his planned candidacy. He insisted in the interview that "whatever one's religion in private life may be, for the office holder, nothing takes precedence over his oath to uphold the Constitution and all its parts—including the First Amendment and the strict separation of Church and State."

Al Smith had made a similar pledge in 1928, to little effect. In 1959 it was Kennedy's fellow Catholics—now more confident of their place in American society—who initially challenged his position. Robert Hoyt, the editor of a diocesan newspaper in Kansas City, argued that Kennedy's willingness to surrender his religious convictions for political gain made him unfit for the Presidency. "If this is an American doctrine," Hoyt fumed over Kennedy's views on church–state relations, "I'm leaving for Tahiti." The Jesuit editor of *America* magazine wrote that Kennedy could not possibly believe that his religion could be kept apart from his politics, "because a man's conscience has a bearing on his public as well as his private life." And an Ohio Catholic newspaper editorialized: "Some day, we should like to see a Catholic, when questioned about the possible conflict between his Church and the Constitution to stand up and say: 'It's none of your business how I feel on these matters. Accept me for what I am, not for what I believe. If you can't do this, then satisfy your prejudice and vote against . . . me.'"

Kennedy quickly sought to mend his relationship with American Catholics. He explained that since he was "trained neither in philosophy, theology, or Church history," he had merely tried to assert, in the *Look* interview, that a Catholic could be a loyal President. After Kennedy won his party's nomination and the 1960 campaign began in earnest, he suddenly faced a much tougher challenge from skeptical or bigoted non-Catholics than from members of his own church. At a meeting of concerned Protestant leaders in Washington, D.C., in September 1960, Norman Vincent Peale, author of the immensely popular book *The Power of Positive Thinking,* declared, "Our American culture is at stake. I don't say it won't survive, but it won't be what it was." The delegates at the meeting, representing 37 Protestant groups, issued a statement that warned, "It is inconceivable that a Roman Catholic president would not be under extreme pressure by the hierarchy of his church to accede to its policies."

The group's anti-Catholic rhetoric backfired. Protestant theologian Reinhold Niebuhr, one of the most respected and influential thinkers of the 20th century, immediately charged that "Dr. Peale and his associates . . . show blind prejudice." Republican candidate Richard M. Nixon pledged to keep religion out of the election campaign. Less than a week after the Washington meeting, Kennedy persuasively asserted, at a meeting of the Greater Houston Ministerial Association, that "I am not the Catholic candidate for President. I am the Democratic Party's candidate for President who happens to be Catholic. I do not speak for the Church on public matters—and the Church does not speak for me."

John F. Kennedy won the Presidency in November 1960 by one of the narrowest margins in history. He readily fulfilled his promise to keep his religious beliefs separate from the execution of his duties as President. Some Catholics hoped that Kennedy might grow in office and find a way to balance his faith and his political leadership in a way that benefited both. His assassination in Dallas on November 22, 1963, not only ended the career of one of the most gifted politicians in American Catholic history but ushered in a period of great turmoil for both the church and the nation.

John F. Kennedy Confronts the Religion Issue

On September 12, 1960, Democratic Presidential nominee John F. Kennedy addressed the Greater Houston Ministerial Association, one of many Protestant bodies deeply concerned about the prospect of a Roman Catholic President. Kennedy was extensively briefed prior to the session by John Cogley, a former editor of the liberal Catholic magazine Commonweal *and a thoughtful commentator on the issue of church–state relations. Kennedy's presentation was widely viewed as highly successful in allaying the ministers' fears about having a Catholic in the White House.*

While the so-called religious issue is necessarily and properly the chief topic here tonight, I want to emphasize from the outset that I believe that we have far more critical issues in the 1960 election; the spread of Communist influence, until it now festers only ninety miles off the coast of Florida—the humiliating treatment of our President and Vice-President by those who no longer respect our power—the hungry children I saw in West Virginia, the old people who cannot pay their doctor's bills, the families forced to give up their farms—an America with too many slums, with too few schools, and too late to the moon and outer space.

These are the real issues which should decide this campaign. And they are not religious issues—for war and hunger and ignorance and despair need no religious barrier.

But because I am a Catholic, and no Catholic has ever been elected President, the real issues in this campaign have been obscured—perhaps deliberately, in some quarters less responsible than this. So it is apparently necessary for me to state once again—not only what kind of church I believe in, for that should be important only to me—but what kind of America I believe in.

I believe in an America where the separation of church and state is absolute—where no Catholic prelate would tell the President (should he be a Catholic) how to act, and no Protestant minister would tell his parishioners for whom to vote—where no church or church school is granted any public funds or political preference—and where no man is denied public office merely because his religion differs from the President who might appoint him or the people who might elect him.

I believe in an America that is officially neither Catholic, Protestant nor Jewish—where no public official either requests or accepts instructions on public policy from the Pope, the National Council of Churches or any other ecclesiastical source—where no religious body seeks to impose its will directly or indirectly upon the general populace or the public acts of its officials—and where religious liberty is so indivisible that an act against one church is treated as an act against all.

For while this year it may be a Catholic against whom the finger of suspicion is pointed, in other years it has been, and may someday be again, a Jew—or a Quaker—or a Unitarian—or a Baptist. It was Virginia's harassment of Baptist preachers, for example, that led to Jefferson's statute of religious freedom. Today, I may be the victim—but tomorrow it may be you—until the whole fabric of our harmonious society is ripped apart at a time of great national peril.

Finally, I believe in an America where religious intolerance will someday end— where all men and all churches are treated as equal—where every man has the same right to attend or not attend the church of his choice—where there is no Catholic vote, no anti-Catholic vote, no bloc voting of any kind—and where Catholics, Protestants and Jews, at both the lay and the pastoral level, will refrain from those attitudes of disdain and division which have so often marred their works in the past, and promote instead the American ideal of brotherhood.

That is the kind of America in which I believe. And it represents the kind of Presidency in which I believe—a great office that must be neither humbled by making it the instrument of any one religious group, nor tarnished by arbitrarily withholding its occupancy from the members of any one religious group. I believe in a President whose religious views are his own private affair, neither imposed by him upon the Nation nor imposed by the Nation upon him as a condition to holding that office. . . .

This is the kind of America I believe in—and this is the kind I fought for in the South Pacific, and the kind my brother died for in Europe. No one suggested then that we might have a "divided loyalty," that we did "not believe in liberty" or that we belonged to a disloyal group that threatened the "freedoms for which our forefathers died."

Chapter 7

The People of God Divided?

n October 1958, Pope Pius XII died after leading the Roman Catholic Church for two eventful decades. The College of Cardinals, the body responsible for electing a new pope, chose as his successor Angelo Roncalli, the popular bishop of Venice, Italy. The cardinals could hardly have selected a man more different from the aloof, aristocratic Pius XII. Roncalli, who reigned as John XXIII, came from a peasant family with 13 children. Despite his background as a papal diplomat in several countries, he was known more for his personal warmth than for political or theological talents. Because he was 76 it was widely assumed that his would merely be a caretaker papacy, filling time until a more viable candidate for a lengthier reign emerged. But just three months after his election, John XXIII shocked the Vatican elite by declaring his intention to convene a general council of the church, the first in nearly a century. (John XXIII named it the Second Vatican Council; the first council of the modern era had been suspended in 1870 after Italian troops entered Rome during the final campaign for that country's unification. The Second Vatican Council became widely known as Vatican II.)

General councils bring together bishops and theologians from around the world to address pressing concerns as they are identified by the leaders of the church. Pope John XXIII explained that "a flash of heavenly light" had inspired him to call the council. He was concerned

The Second Vatican Council opened on October 11, 1962, with a ceremony at St. Peter's Basilica in Rome. More than 3,000 bishops and theologians from around the world participated in Vatican II.

141

that the Vatican bureaucracy had grown out of touch with the spiritual needs of the world's Catholics, and he also desired a "strengthening of religious unity" among different Christian traditions. Vatican II met for four sessions between 1962 and 1965 and produced 16 major documents. (John XXIII died in June 1963 and was succeeded by Pope Paul VI, who shared many of his predecessor's desires for reform of the church.)

The council document of greatest immediate concern to American Catholics was the "Declaration on Religious Liberty," whose principle author was John Courtney Murray, a Maryland Jesuit well known for his pioneering work in formulating a modern theory of church–state relations. This document asserted that all human beings were entitled to "freedom or immunity from coercion in religious matters"; this right was to be properly safeguarded by the civil authorities. The Declaration represented a major shift in the church's position on church and state, because it had customarily demanded the right to enjoy special privileges in societies where the church was historically dominant. This document signaled the church's implicit approval of the American experiment in religious pluralism, in which the government recognized the freedom of worship for all groups but favored none. It also represented a personal triumph for John Courtney Murray, who had long argued that American democracy was fully compatible with Catholicism. Murray's views were similar to and updated those held by "Americanist" Catholics in the late 19th century.

Vatican II ushered in one of the most exciting, if controversial, periods in the entire history of the Roman Catholic Church. Many of the sweeping changes associated with the council—such as the replacement of Latin with the vernacular, or local language, in the liturgy—were called for in council documents but implemented and expanded by subsequent directives. Most American Catholics were inspired more by the spirit of reform emerging from the council than by the substance of the documents themselves. One dramatic innovation of the council was unmistakable, however: the church community was now defined as making up "the People of God," an image that was highly appealing to citizens of a democracy such as the United States. Catholics were encouraged to focus not on the aspects of their faith that divided them from others but to embrace charitably the modern world and its diverse cultures.

The resulting changes in American Catholic life were swift and deep. Sister Jacqueline Grennan of the Sisters of Loretto, a religious community founded by pioneer women in Kentucky in 1812, declared in 1964 that it was time for religious orders to "do something about these medieval habits [religious attire] so that we can again assume our citizenship, and that we may, on the free and open market, again volunteer to make our investment in the mainstream of American society." Asserting that she wanted "only to be a *worldly* nun," Grennan, who served as president of the Sisters of Loretto's Webster College near St. Louis, persuaded her community in 1967 to "laicize" the school, or remove it from the control of its sponsoring order. She subsequently left the Sisters of Loretto, married, and assumed the presidency of Hunter College, a branch of the City University of New York.

In Los Angeles, the leaders of the Immaculate Heart of Mary congregation incurred the wrath of Cardinal Francis McIntyre when, in 1967, they announced a plan to institute "liberal changes" in their rule and lifestyle. These changes gave sisters the right to choose careers other than teaching and to exert a greater voice in the governance of individual convents. Sister Corita Kent, a well-known teacher and "pop" artist (a movement associated with Andy Warhol that drew inspiration from the materials of everyday life, including consumer goods), had declared in 1965 that if a religious community prevented a woman from "being beautiful and human and Christian, that community must be remade over and over again."

Although Jacqueline Grennan and Corita Kent were exceptionally vivid personalities, in the 1960s many ordinary Catholics reexamined their own commitment to the church in light of Vatican II. The vexing

Jacqueline Wexler (center), formerly Sister Jacqueline Grennan, at an Alumni Hall of Fame reception at Hunter College in 1974. As college president, she was on the committee that selected Gertrude Groden (left) and Pauli Murray for induction.

More than 150 Catholic priests participated in a sit-in outside the 1968 National Conference of Catholic Bishops in Washington, D.C. The demonstration was staged to show support for the local priests who were disciplined by Cardinal O'Boyle for public dissent on the birth control issue.

issue of religious authority, which the council had presumably broadened in stressing the importance of dialogue among bishops, pastors, and members of the laity exploded in 1968 when Pope Paul VI issued the encyclical *Humanae Vitae* ("Of Human Life"). In 1963, Pope John XXIII had appointed a special commission to examine the church's teachings on the use of artificial contraception. The progesterone birth control pill developed in the 1950s had proved to offer medical benefits to some women who were not trying to avoid pregnancy but suffered from irregular menstrual cycles. Applying the church's traditional moral reasoning to the issue, some theologians concluded that the pill was acceptable in cases where the prevention of pregnancy was a secondary effect of its intended use.

John Rock, a Catholic doctor who was codeveloper of the birth control pill, further argued that the pill aided women using the "rhythm" method, the one form of family planning accepted by the church because it was based on abstinence from sex during a woman's monthly fertile period. By regulating the menstrual cycle, the birth control pill enabled women to know when they were ovulating, the time when those using the rhythm method abstained from sexual intercourse.

The birth control pill was of course chemically designed to prevent pregnancy altogether, so its use could not really be said to aid in "natural" family planning. Some theologians, and many married couples, argued that human sexuality was a gift from God that was intended not only for procreation but also to increase the "mutual love" of a husband and wife. The debate over birth control exposed a broader crisis of church authority, at a time when more and more women and men were choosing to make their own decisions on matters they now viewed as private and personal.

Following the death of Pope John XXIII, Pope Paul VI added married couples and experts on population issues to the commission, which in 1966 voted 52 to 4 in favor of ending the church's ban on artificial contraception. A panel of bishops then voted in favor of several propositions that offered support for the panel's recommendations. The pope, however, concluded in *Humanae Vitae* that "the natural law . . . teaches as absolutely required that in any use of marriage whatever there must be no impairment of its natural capacity to procreate human life."

The pope's reaffirmation of the ban on contraception led to the gravest crisis of authority the church had faced in centuries. While theologians debated the issue, the use of contraception by American Catholic women increased from an estimated 30 percent in 1955 to 68 percent by 1970. In 1964 Rosemary Ruether, a young theologian, created a sensation when the *Saturday Evening Post* published her article "Speaking Out: A Catholic Mother Tells Why I Believe in Birth Control." When *Humanae Vitae* was issued in 1968, many priests chose to ignore it, while others argued that the pope was not speaking infallibly in this instance and Catholics were therefore free to challenge the teaching. In Washington, D.C., Archbishop Patrick A. O'Boyle disciplined 51 priests who openly dissented over *Humanae Vitae.* Forced to recant in order to be allowed to resume their priestly duties, nearly half the men eventually left the priesthood.

Defections from the ranks of the priesthood and sisterhood increased dramatically in the late 1960s. The dissent over *Humanae Vitae* was probably more a symptom than a cause in that it highlighted the gulf between the Vatican's conservative position on moral issues and the dramatic changes in American social attitudes during this period, especially those concerning human sexuality. Many American priests and nuns now decided they wished to marry, while others concluded that the church's claims of authority violated their personal freedom. In 1966, some 200 American priests resigned from the active ministry, a number that had grown to 750 by 1969, while the number of ordinations in the same period dropped by more than 15 percent. And the rate of decline increased over time: whereas in 1964 there were 47,500 seminarians in training for the priesthood, by 1984 there would be approximately 12,000. Two hundred Catholic seminaries closed their doors during these two decades. In 1966 there were roughly 180,000 nuns in the United States. By 1980 the number had dwindled to less than 130,000, despite a significant increase in the Catholic population during the same period.

While the sexual revolution of the 1960s contributed to the alienation of many Catholics from their church, the Vietnam War led others to offer a witness against war, violence, and racism that was deeply rooted in their faith commitments. In his 1963 encyclical *Pacem in Terris* ("Peace on Earth"), Pope John XXIII asserted that "it is hardly possible to imagine that in the atomic era war could be used as an instrument of peace." The pope went on to state that if civil authorities acted in violation of "the will of God, neither the laws made nor the authorizations granted can be binding on the conscience of the citizens." Inspired by the pope's words, a small group of Catholics led the first protests directed specifically against U.S. military intervention in Vietnam. In the summer of 1963, before the first U.S. combat forces had been sent to Vietnam, Tom Cornell and Christopher Kearns of the Catholic Worker movement demonstrated in New York against American aid to the regime in South Vietnam. "We got on coast to coast television," Cornell recalled. "That sparked other things, so it was something of a coup."

In August 1965, Kearns was pictured burning his draft card in a *Life* magazine layout, an action that prompted the passage of a federal law making similar acts punishable by five years in a federal prison. In October of that year David Miller, a member of the New York Catholic Worker community, became the first person to burn his own draft card publicly in defiance of the new law. In November, Cornell and six others, including a fellow Catholic Worker, burned their draft cards in front of 1,500 onlookers in Manhattan's Union Square. Already well aware of the importance of media coverage at demonstrations, Cornell and the others "timed it for the Sunday papers. A guy infiltrated the crowd and squirted us with a fire extinguisher. Just water, thank God. That made a very impressive photo. Again it caused a sensation. . . . It made an enormous impact."

David Miller of the Catholic Worker movement burns his military classification card in a 1965 antiwar protest held outside the Armed Services Induction Center in New York. Many Americans both inside and outside the church were surprised by the intensity of the Catholic antiwar movement in the 1960s.

Just three days later, on November 9, a 21-year-old former seminarian from upstate New York, Roger LaPorte, set himself afire in front of the United Nations building on the East Side of Manhattan. As he was being taken to the nearby Bellevue Hospital, where he later died, LaPorte explained: "I am a Catholic Worker. I am antiwar. I did this as a religious action." LaPorte's suicide sent shock waves through the burgeoning Catholic peace movement, and brought to the forefront of the movement Father Daniel Berrigan, a 44-year-old Jesuit who had taught LaPorte at LeMoyne College in Syracuse. Along with his younger brother Philip, a Josephite priest (the Josephites are known for their service to African-American communities), Daniel Berrigan had been involved in the civil rights movement since the late 1950s. He converted to pacifism partly through his contacts with Dorothy Day but especially with Thomas Merton, who—from his cinder-block cabin on the grounds of his Kentucky monastery—had written a series of articles condemning war in the *Catholic Worker*.

At a memorial service for Roger LaPorte, Daniel Berrigan preached that the young man "gave his life, so that others might live." Berrigan's remarks outraged New York's Cardinal Francis Spellman, a staunch supporter of the U.S. military campaign in Vietnam. As a Jesuit of the New

Father Philip Berrigan flashes the peace sign to supporters from behind bars at a prison in Harrisburg, Pennsylvania. Berrigan was among a group of eight antiwar activists accused of plotting to kidnap Secretary of State Henry Kissinger. They were freed when a mistrial was declared in 1972.

York Province rather than a parish (or "diocesan") priest (the American Jesuit community, like some other religious orders, is divided into territorial "provinces") Berrigan was not technically under Spellman's authority, but the cardinal persuaded Berrigan's Jesuit superiors to punish him for failing to condemn LaPorte's suicide as a violation of Catholic moral teaching. Berrigan was exiled to Latin America for several months, where he grew even more determined to offer a personal witness against violence and war.

On returning to the United States in 1966, Berrigan discovered that his brother Philip had rejected conventional pacifism and was preparing to take direct action against the government for waging war in Vietnam. In 1967 Philip Berrigan led a small group of activists that contemplated blowing up a building in Baltimore (while it was unoccupied) that housed thousands of draft files on young men eligible for the armed services. Berrigan was advised by a concerned attorney to make a symbolic gesture instead, such as pouring blood or paint into the locks protecting the building from intruders. Accordingly, he and three members of the Interfaith Peace Mission entered the draft board office on October 27, 1967, poured blood on the files in front of horrified clerks and members of the news media (although they had been tipped off in advance of the action, a photographer from the *Baltimore Sun* became so upset that he fainted), then waited patiently to be arrested.

The Baltimore Four, as the group came to be known, would spawn the Milwaukee Fourteen, the Catonsville Nine, and other groups of Catholic radicals who took nonviolent action in the name of peace. This new Catholic Left played a major role in the much broader protest movement against the Vietnam War, drawing national attention to conflicts within the church that only intensified as the 1960s wore on. On May 17,

1968, six weeks after the assassination of Dr. Martin Luther King, Jr., in Memphis, Daniel and Philip Berrigan and seven associates raided the draft board office in Catonsville, Maryland, burning hundreds of files with homemade napalm (as a protest against the use of the jellied gasoline substance in Vietnam, which sometimes left civilians horribly burned) before they were arrested. Less than three weeks later, Robert F. Kennedy, a senator from New York and brother of the slain President, won the California Democratic primary in his bid to gain the party's Presidential nomination. Kennedy defeated Minnesota senator Eugene J. McCarthy, a one-time seminarian at a Benedictine monastery who, along with his wife, Abigail, had been deeply attracted to the Catholic Rural Life movement (a branch of Catholic Action) in Minnesota in the 1940s. Moments after making his victory speech, Robert Kennedy was shot and killed as he was leaving Los Angeles's Ambassador Hotel.

The Trappist monk Thomas Merton, who Robert Kennedy had tried to bring to the White House for a visit shortly after John F. Kennedy was assassinated, wrote in his journal that 1968 was proving to be a "brute of a year." Robert Kennedy's devoutly Catholic wife, Ethel Kennedy, had begun a correspondence with Merton in the early 1960s in which he wrote of his strong opposition to America's growing nuclear arsenal. Robert Kennedy was clearly influenced by the Catholic peace movement, as well as by his association in the last years of his life with César Chávez, the Mexican-American leader of the migrant farm workers' movement in California.

Chávez was born near Yuma, Arizona, in 1927. When he was 12 years old his family was forced off their small farm and entered the migrant labor force after they were unable to pay taxes on the property. Following a stint in the U. S. Navy, Chávez, his wife, Helen, and their young family (which grew to include eight children) settled in the Mexican-American section of San Jose, California, where he found work in a lumberyard.

In the early 1950s César Chávez was introduced to the social teachings of the church by Donald McDonnell, a San Francisco priest who worked as part of a mission team serving migrant field workers. "He told me about social justice and the Church's stand on farm labor and reading

Cesar Chavez's work on behalf of migrant farm workers was strongly supported by leading figures in the church. In this 1973 photograph Chavez (center) is pictured with Bishop James S. Rausch (left), General Secretary of the United States Catholic Conference, and Monsignor George G. Higgins, consultant to the Bishops' Committee on Farm Labor.

from the encyclicals of Pope Leo XIII, in which he upheld labor unions." In 1962, after working in voter registration and citizenship campaigns, Chávez established the National Farm Workers Association with the assistance of Dolores Huerta, a Mexican-American community organizer from Stockton, California. In 1965 the NFWA joined a strike against table grape growers in Delano, California, that had been launched by a largely Filipino-American agricultural workers union. In the course of the five-year strike the two groups merged to form the United Farm Workers Association. The celebration of mass became a central feature of gatherings of *La Causa* (the cause), a nonviolent movement to win recognition of the union by employers. Chávez helped introduce Americans to some of the themes associated with the "liberation theology" movement that emerged in Latin America in the mid-1960s. Liberation theologians argued that the church had for too long defended the rights of the wealthy. It was the obligation of Christians, they insisted, to identify with the poor and oppressed, even if the privileged status enjoyed by the church itself was placed in jeopardy.

On February 15, 1968, César Chávez went on a hunger strike as penance for violent acts committed during his union's struggle for survival. He did not eat for 25 days, attended daily Mass and prayed for the movement's re-dedication to nonviolence. When he broke the fast in March, Robert Kennedy traveled to California to participate in a Mass of Thanksgiving. At communion Chávez and Kennedy shared a piece of the consecrated bread.

Chávez's recollection of the crowd that swarmed around Kennedy indicates that Mexican Americans viewed Kennedy—as they did Chávez himself—as a spiritual as well as political leader. "His hands were scratched where people were trying to touch him," said Chávez. "You could see the blood." During the victory celebration in Los Angeles on the night Kennedy was killed, the crowd at the Ambassador Hotel cried out not only "We Want Kennedy" but "We Want Chávez."

The terrible violence of the spring of 1968 produced one of the gravest crises in American history. Among Catholics, who were unaccustomed to finding themselves at the forefront of political and social concerns shared by the entire nation, the strains were taking a heavy toll. Then on December 10, Thomas Merton, who enjoyed perhaps the greatest stature of any spiritual figure of his generation, was electrocuted by a malfunctioning fan in Bangkok, Thailand, as he stepped out of a shower stall. Merton had been given permission to travel from the Abbey of Gethsemani to Southeast Asia to participate in an international conference on monasticism. Merton's remains were flown home in an airplane carrying the bodies of U.S. servicemen killed in the war he and many of his admirers had attempted to stop, through the power of prayer and Christian witness. When Daniel Berrigan learned of Merton's death, he "really was in anguish," recalled a friend. "He felt like Merton was the other part of him, that they'd been through so much together, that they'd helped each other stay priests."

Three months earlier, Daniel Berrigan had been sentenced to three years in federal prison for his role in the Catonsville draft board raid. While free on bond he fled, to delay serving his sentence. For four months the Federal Bureau of Investigation made his arrest and capture one of its top priorities. Berrigan was finally apprehended on Block Island, off the Rhode Island coast, in August 1970 by FBI agents disguised as birdwatchers. By that time a Catholic backlash against the well-publicized activities of the Berrigans and other Catholic radicals was under way. (One of the Catholic FBI agents who arrested Daniel and Philip Berrigan after the Catonsville action disgustedly remarked, "I'm changing my religion.") Many Catholics were confused or horrified by the new activism of so many priests and sisters.

The novelist Jack Kerouac, so often associated with youthful rebelliousness, declared shortly before his death in 1969 that he would gladly serve in Vietnam in the (highly unlikely) event his services were needed. Kerouac became an admirer of the conservative Catholic pundit William F. Buckley, whose magazine *National Review* was a prime critic of the Catholic Left. Kerouac spoke for many products of the immigrant church when he remarked, in 1969, "I'm pro-American and the radical political involvements seem to tend elsewhere. . . . The country gave my Canadian family a good break, more or less, and we see no reason to demean said country."

The turmoil and confusion within the church were reflected in national politics. A substantial number of northern Catholics who had voted initially for the liberal Robert Kennedy during the primary season of 1968 voted later that year for the right-wing former governor of Alabama, George Wallace, who ran on a third-party ticket in the November general election. Wallace, who was best known for physically barring the entry of black students to the University of Alabama in 1963, had almost nothing in common with Catholic voters other than a shared concern that traditional American values were being eroded by public immorality and disrespect for authority. When Wallace remarked during the campaign that he "spoke better Polish" than the other candidates, he was referring not to his linguistic abilities but to his new-found cultural bonds with northern ethnic Catholics.

The defection of many Catholics from their traditional loyalty to the Democrats enabled Richard M. Nixon to squeak past Hubert H. Humphrey to gain the Presidency in 1968. Nixon immediately went to work building a base constituency of conservative Americans he called "the silent majority," distinguishing them from a vocal minority of liberal and radical critics of his administration. Nixon even championed the "ethnic revival" of the early 1970s, which saw large numbers of primarily third-generation, middle- and working-class Catholics seek to rediscover their roots in the immigrant experience. The new ethnicity further alienated many Catholics from the Democratic party, which was in the midst of a reform process that ultimately reduced the power of big-city "machine" politicians in favor of greater representation for women and members of racial minorities. In 1972, when Nixon trounced Democratic challenger George McGovern, a higher percentage of Catholics voted Republican than in any other national election in American history.

Although the ethnic revival of the 1970s was initially focused on white ethnic communities from European backgrounds (and African Americans, especially after the phenomenal success of *Roots,* a 1976 television program that traced a family's history from Africa to southern slavery to freedom), other ethnic groups—some new, some long overlooked—were helping transform American Catholicism. Mexican Americans, who had been overwhelmingly concentrated in the rural Southwest prior to 1900, began moving to large urban centers in the 1920s. The Mexican-American population of Los Angeles tripled in that decade to nearly 100,000. By the 1930s sizable communities of Mexican-Americans (more than 90 percent Roman Catholic) could be found in industrial cities as far north as Chicago and Detroit. Although Mexican Americans generally worshiped in national parishes, a shortage of priests from their homeland and the desire of church leaders to promote Americanization resulted in a blending of traditions. As the memoirist Richard Rodriguez explained in *Days of Obligation* of his childhood in Sacramento, California, "I was a Mexican teenager in America who had become an Irish Catholic."

In the late 1960s and 1970s, however, a renewal of pride in Mexican-American culture emerged, symbolized by the adoption of the formerly somewhat undesirable term Chicano by many members of this community. Inspired by the example of Farm Workers' Union leader César Chávez, Catholic Chicanos sought to merge the devotional practices of

Our Lady of Guadalupe, the preeminent icon for Latin Americans, is known as Mother of the Americas. She has also been adopted by pro-life groups as "protectress of the unborn."

traditional Mexican religion with a commitment to social action.

Our Lady of Guadalupe served as the main symbol of this cause. In 1971 a Chicano theologian from San Antonio, Father Virgilio Elizondo, helped establish the Mexican American Cultural Center, which provides training for both clergy and members of the laity interested in a deeper appreciation of Mexican-American culture and spirituality. In 1970 Father Patricio Flores became the first Mexican-American bishop with his appointment as auxiliary bishop of San Antonio. Cesar Chávez read a scripture passage at a Mass celebrating Bishop Flores' ordination, an event attended by 8,000 people. Bishop Flores later served as bishop of El Paso, Texas, before returning to San Antonio as its first Hispanic archbishop. By the mid-1990s there were 12 Mexican-American bishops in the United States.

When Cuban insurgents led by Fidel Castro overthrew the unpopular dictatorship of Fulgencio Batista in 1959, most residents of that island nation 90 miles south of the tip of Florida welcomed the change in government. Castro's repressive Communist regime, however, caused more than 155,000 Cubans to flee their homeland between 1959 and 1962. Most of these refugees settled in the Miami area, but large communities of Cuban Americans are now also found in Hudson County, New Jersey. Many of these exiles had been landholders, shopkeepers, or professionals in Cuba and were able to build a strong network of civic, political, and religious activities in the United States. The antireligious policies of the Castro government caused many Cuban Americans to develop a stronger attachment to the church than they had known in their homeland. Cuban Americans in Miami even reestablished the Jesuit *Colegio de Belen,* a school once attended by Castro himself.

Prior to the 1940s, few natives of Puerto Rico lived on the American mainland. By 1950 more than 300,000 Puerto Ricans had migrated northward, with the vast majority settling in New York City, drawn there by employment opportunities and the availability of relatively affordable airfares between San Juan and New York (Puerto Rican residents are citizens of the United States). Cardinal Francis Spellman decided to integrate this new community into territorial parishes rather than establish national parishes, as had been the custom for earlier immigrant groups. In 1956 Spellman did, however, authorize a young priest, Ivan Illich, to establish an institute at the Catholic University of Puerto Rico designed to immerse non-Latino American priests in the Spanish language and Puerto Rican culture. Ironically, many of the priests trained at the center became so committed to winning social justice for Puerto Ricans in New York that many of their parishioners looked instead to more traditional forms of Spanish piety.

Many Puerto Rican Catholics participated in the *cursillo* (Spanish for "little course") movement, a spiritual renewal program begun by a group of laymen on the Spanish island of Majorca in 1949. The *cursillo*, a program of shared prayer, reading, and discussion, focuses intensively on

Cuban Americans in Miami mark the end of the Christmas season by celebrating the Feast of the Three Kings each year on January 6th. The festival and parade are an important feature of Cuban-American life in south Florida.

155

Christ as the center of all spiritual life and the living model for all human activity. The *cursillo* also played a key role in the Catholic Charismatic Renewal movement founded in 1967 by students and faculty at two Catholic universities—Duquesne, in Pittsburgh, and Notre Dame, in Indiana—and staff members of a student parish at Michigan State University.

Derived from the Greek word for "gifted," charismatic Christianity is rooted in a conviction that the Holy Spirit bestows upon the faithful such special gifts as healing or the ability to speak in tongues (also known as "glossolalia"). Catholic charismatics share much in common with Protestant Pentecostals (from the Greek word for "fiftieth," marking the number of days after Easter on which the Holy Spirit appeared to Christ's apostles; they are described in the Bible's Book of Acts as having "tongues as of fire, distributed and resting on each one of them"). When the charismatic revival grew dramatically in the early 1970s, church leaders became concerned that it might threaten to blur the distinction between Catholic and Protestant forms of worship. In 1976, however, the church cautiously approved the movement, and Catholic charismatics demonstrated fervent loyalty to Pope John Paul II in the 1980s and 1990s, though the movement was then less conspicuous than in its early days.

While many Latino Catholics participated in the charismatic renewal, the movement was dominated by white, middle-class suburbanites. Large numbers of Latinos came to feel alienated from the church in general by the 1970s: though the statistics are a matter of intense debate, it is estimated that between 10 and 25 percent of Hispanic Catholics have since the 1970s left the church to join free-standing evangelical and Pentecostal congregations operated by members of their local communities. By the 1990s fewer than 60 percent of Hispanic high school seniors identified themselves as Catholics. Yet if Latinos are classified as one subgroup within American Catholicism, they make up the largest ethnic community in the church. This method of classification is highly questionable, however, because the Latino population in America is highly diverse and becoming more so as the 1980s and 1990s continued to see a significant influx of Colombians, Dominicans, Guatemalans, and Nicaraguans.

Asian-American Catholics also represent a diverse array of cultural traditions. Like Latinos, Filipino Americans came to the United States from a land that was once a Spanish colony. The first Filipino Americans were sailors who fled their masters in the Spanish navy and settled in the New Orleans area. Filipinos did not migrate to the U.S. mainland in large numbers, however, until the years after World War II. In part because a significant portion of the Filipino immigrant community was English speaking (their homeland had been under American protectorate status since 1898), Filipino Catholics generally blended into existing urban parishes. Filipino-American Catholicism has made an important impact not only in areas of southern California but in Jersey City, New Jersey, and other eastern urban settings.

Filipinos make up the only Asian-American community that is predominantly Roman Catholic, but members of other national groups have made a major contribution to the church in America. The decade following the end of the Vietnam War in 1975 saw a massive exodus of refugees to Canada, Australia, and especially the United States, where more than 1 million Vietnamese resided by the 1990s. The Vietnamese-American Catholic community, more than 250,000 strong, quickly organized tightly knit parishes in such locations as Orange County, California; New Orleans, Louisiana; and in the Houston, Texas, area. This community is served by 400 Vietnamese priests representing numerous religious orders, including the Congregation of Mary Corredemptrix, which was founded by a Vietnamese priest in Carthage, Missouri, and

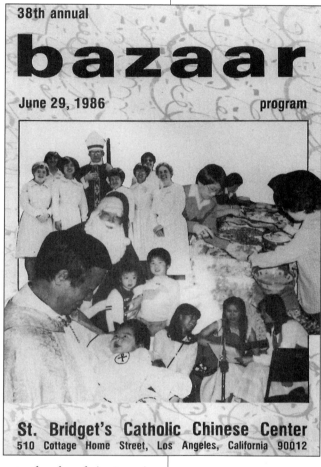

38th annual

bazaar

June 29, 1986   program

St. Bridget's Catholic Chinese Center
510 Cottage Home Street, Los Angeles, California 90012

The program cover for the 1986 annual bazaar at St. Bridget's Catholic Chinese Center in Los Angeles shows members in a variety of traditional church activities, including the potluck supper. The visit to Santa is an exception, being a cultural rather than religious tradition.

sponsors an annual religious celebration attended by 30,000 people. The Lovers of the Cross, a women's religious community founded in Vietnam in the French colonial era, is the largest of nearly 20 female religious congregations (most quite small) that play an important role in Vietnamese-American religious life.

Vietnamese Americans, along with the members of all recent immigrant communities, struggle to maintain their cultural traditions for themselves and their children in the face of intense competition from secular consumer culture. The desire of Vietnamese Catholics to worship in national parishes has sometimes produced conflict with church officials: in 1986 a group of parishioners occupied Our Lady Queen of Martyrs Mission in San Jose, California, for 10 months after the local bishop removed a popular pastor. The group accused the bishop of trying to "assimilate them quickly into the mainstream," a charge he denied. The issue of national parishes remained highly complicated into the 1990s as the notion of integration—which played such a central role in the civil rights movement of the 1950s and 1960s—was challenged by advocates of multiculturalism, who insisted that the church must learn to celebrate its many diverse traditions.

In the 1970s and 1980s American Catholics continued to debate the meaning of Vatican II as the church in the United States grew more fragmented than at any time in its history. The fault lines in the church reflected divisions within society at large. The struggle of women for full equality in the 1970s, symbolized by the drive for ratification of the Equal Rights Amendment (ERA) to the U.S. Constitution, saw Catholics play leading roles on both sides of the issue. Although the National Council of Catholic Women (an organization closely tied to the National Catholic Welfare Conference) opposed the measure in the 1970s—as it had since the ERA was first proposed in the 1920s—the National Coalition of Nuns (with a membership of over 1,300) and the National Conference of Catholic Charities supported the ERA. A Massachusetts Congresswoman, Margaret O'Shaughnessy Heckler, who had received a Catholic education from kindergarten through law school, was a leading proponent of the

ERA. Phyllis Schlafly, a devout Catholic from St. Louis, became a celebrity for her impassioned crusade to defeat the ERA, which she feared would compel the church to ordain women as priests.

In 1973, in the case of *Roe* v. *Wade,* the U.S. Supreme Court ruled that state laws banning abortion (termination of pregnancy by a method that destroys a fetus while in the womb) were unconstitutional. The extremely controversial issue of abortion—and the Catholic Church's forceful opposition to legalized abortion—did not produce a great deal of open dissent within the church, unlike the issue of artificial contraception. In the 1970s and 1980s, in fact, abortion was a focal point of much organized Catholic activism on the grassroots level, where women and men played leading roles in the right-to-life movement. Advocates of the

A Florida woman holds her sleeping daughter as she prays during the 1998 National Prayer Vigil for Life. Several thousand Catholics prayed for an end to abortion during the nightlong vigil at the Basilica of the National Shrine of the Immaculate Conception in Washington, D.C.

pro-life position argue that human life begins at conception or shortly thereafter: they therefore view abortion as the taking of innocent life. Advocates of the pro-choice position maintain that women possess the right to decide whether to bear a child or terminate pregnancy.

The abortion issue also caused bishops and theologians to renew the church's traditional beliefs on a host of moral issues. In the early 1980s Archbishop Joseph Bernardin of Chicago proposed that the Catholic defense of the unborn was part of a philosophy he depicted as "the seamless web of life," a conviction that all human life was sacred and that society did not have the right to execute convicted murderers any more than to permit abortion.

Occasionally the abortion issue pitted church officials against Catholic politicians who argued that in a pluralist society—one that includes a wide array of religious and cultural traditions—the teachings of the church might not always prevail in the public arena. In 1984 New York governor Mario Cuomo was strongly criticized by Archbishop (later Cardinal) John J. O'Connor for refusing to veto a bill permitting public funding of abortions. Cuomo, who was widely viewed as a possible future contender for the Democratic party's Presidential nomination, decided to tackle the issue of abortion and politics directly in a speech at the University of Notre Dame in September 1984. There he argued that "the Catholic who holds political office in a pluralistic democracy . . . bears special responsibility . . . to help create conditions . . . where everyone who chooses may hold beliefs different from specifically Catholic ones— sometimes even contradictory to them."

Governor Cuomo further asserted in that speech that "as a Catholic, I have accepted certain answers as the right ones for myself and for my family," including a belief that abortion was morally wrong. He viewed the persistence of abortion not as "a failure of government" that could be solved by laws but as the result of choices made by individuals, Catholic and non-Catholic alike. He saw his vocation as a Catholic politician not so much entailing "trying to make laws for other people, but by living the laws already written for us by God, in our minds and hearts." Critics noted that Cuomo seemed to divorce his own convictions from the moral judgments he was inevitably called upon to make in his role as governor, while his supporters insisted that only by participating fully in dialogue with those holding different convictions could Catholics make a contribution to the broader society.

While a very small number of Catholics openly dissented from the church's opposition to abortion, public opinion research data affirmed Mario Cuomo's contention that the range of Catholic attitudes toward abortion closely reflected that of the general public. Such polls were flawed, because they did not take into account the respondents' degree of involvement in church activities, but they did confirm an important trend of the 1970s and 1980s. These same polls, however, revealed that Americans remained highly ambivalent about abortion itself. A CNN/USA Today/Gallup Poll taken in May 1999 indicated that 55 percent of Americans believed that abortion should be permitted only in cases of rape, incest, or to save the life of the mother, while just 16 percent thought it should be illegal under all circumstances. In any case, more and more American Catholics were choosing for themselves which aspects of church doctrine they would accept while rejecting those in which they did not believe. Survey data showed that 30 percent of Catholics believed that it was not necessary to accept the church's position on abortion to remain a "good Catholic," whereas 49 percent did not believe that a good Catholic must attend mass on a weekly basis, despite clear church teaching to the contrary.

The 1980s saw a lively debate within the church over such important issues as nuclear weapons policy and the relationship between the American economic system and the quest for social justice on a global scale. In May 1983 the National Conference of Catholic Bishops issued a pastoral letter, *The Challenge of Peace: God's Promise and Our Response,* which sharply challenged a defense policy based on the threat of nuclear retaliation against the Soviet Union or other foreign powers that might threaten the United States with weapons of mass destruction. Such prominent laypersons as the conservative pundits William F. Buckley and Michael

Novak argued that America's nuclear arsenal served to deter the aggressive intentions of the nation's adversaries. In 1986 the bishops issued the letter *Economic Justice for All,* which argued that in an increasingly global economic environment American capitalism was responsible for suffering and injustice in underdeveloped societies. Novak and William Simon—a wealthy financier and secretary of the Treasury under President Ronald Reagan—responded that the creation of wealth through free markets was the best means available to expand prosperity and promote human dignity around the world.

As the embodiment of the church's teaching authority, the bishops grew accustomed to routine challenges from the right, the left, and even the center in the waning years of the 20th century. Some argued that Catholics now felt free to embrace the aspects of church teaching with which they agreed while ignoring others. "Cafeteria Catholicism," as this brand of selective faith became known, signaled a major shift within the church. From the onset of the "immigrant church" in the 1830s until the aftermath of Vatican II, the American Catholic church had grown more cohesive, better organized, and more effective in drawing boundaries of acceptable practice and behavior than any other Christian denomination. This feat had been accomplished at the same time that Catholics had largely succeeded in gaining full acceptance as Americans. By the 1990s it appeared that Catholics truly were "like everyone else" in the United States, but it was not entirely clear just what made them Catholic. Father Andrew Greeley, a sociologist and best-selling novelist, strongly argued that Catholics possess a unique religious imagination that sets them apart from others. Greeley asserted that young Catholics develop a view of the world as filled with God's grace from the stories they hear, particularly those told by members of their family. In the public arena, however, Catholics applied their religious views in very diverse ways. Conservative Catholics often found themselves in alliances with evangelical Protestants (whose forebears had often denied that Catholics were even Christians), while liberals found much in common with secularists who were deeply suspicious of Catholic political power.

In 1994 the nation's 60 million Roman Catholics accounted for nearly one-quarter of the population of the United States. While occupational and social mobility had resulted in the dispersal of Catholics to all parts of the country, members of the church remained highly concentrated in the older urban regions of the Northeast and Upper Midwest. While Catholics made up 64 percent of Rhode Island's population, for example, they accounted for just 3 percent of Tennessee's inhabitants. The church was experiencing its most rapid growth in the Southwest and southern California, where recent immigrants from Latin America had made the archdiocese of Los Angeles the nation's largest by far, with a Catholic population of more than 3.5 million.

As the 20th century drew to a close, Catholics in America continued to adapt creatively to changing circumstances. In Saginaw, Michigan, a Czech-American nun, Sister Honora Remes, served as "pastoral administrator" of St. Mary's parish. Because of the great shortage of priests, such pastoral administrators—who perform all the duties of a priest other than celebrating mass and administering the sacraments—have been called upon to lead more than 300 American parishes. At the same time, many younger Catholics longed for a revival of traditionalist religion, favoring a renewed emphasis on the church's teaching authority which, they hoped, would lead to a church as unified as that known by their grandparents in the 1930s and 1940s. Yet as the study of American Catholic history shows, diversity has always been the hallmark of the church and its people. A search for unity might well begin with a celebration of this diversity.

Do you have a call waiting?

Thought about *answering* it?

The Sisters of Mercy Women religious who respond to God's call each day through service, prayer, and community life.

The sharp decline in numbers of American Catholic women entering religious life has led several communities to launch innovative promotional campaigns. The number of American sisters fell from 180,000 in 1965 to 83,000 in 1999; during this time their median age rose to 68.

The American Bishops Speak Out on Economic Injustice

In 1986 an informal committee of Catholic bishops headed by Rembert Weakland, Archbishop of Milwaukee, made an intensive study of the U.S. economy in light of the moral and social teachings of the church. The bishops' pastoral letter drew on the tradition of Catholic social teaching. It also reflected the special concern for the poor and the dispossessed that characterized the church in the decades following Vatican II.

The pastoral letter is not a blueprint for the American economy. It does not embrace any particular theory of how the economy works, nor does it attempt to resolve the disputes between different schools of economic thought. Instead, our letter turns to Scripture and to the social teachings of the Church. There, we discover what our economic life must serve, what standards it must meet. Let us examine some of these basic moral principles.

Every economic decision and institution must be judged in light of whether it protects or undermines the dignity of the human person. The pastoral letter begins with the human person. We believe the person is sacred—the clearest reflection of God among us. Human dignity comes from God, not from nationality, race, sex, economic status, or any human accomplishment. We judge any economic system by what it does *for* and *to* people and by how it permits all to *participate* in it. The economy should serve people, not the other way around.

Human dignity can be realized and protected only in community. In our teaching, the human person is not only sacred but also social. How we organize our society—in economics and politics, in law and policy—directly affects human dignity and the capacity of individuals to grow in community. The obligation to "love our neighbor" has an individual dimension, but it also requires a broader social commitment to the common good. We have many partial ways to measure and debate the health of our economy: Gross National Product, per capita income, stock market prices, and so forth. The Christian vision of economic life looks beyond them all and asks, Does economic life enhance or threaten our life together as a community?

All people have a right to participate in the economic life of society. Basic justice demands that people be assured a minimum level of participation in the economy. It is wrong for a person or group to be excluded unfairly or to be unable to participate or contribute to the economy. For example, people who are both able and willing, but cannot get a job are deprived of the participation that is so vital to human development. For, it is through employment that most individuals and families meet their material needs, exercise their talents, and have an opportunity to contribute to the larger community. Such participation has a special significance in our tradition because we believe that it is a means by which we join in carrying forward God's creative activity.

All members of society have a special obligation to the poor and vulnerable. From the Scriptures and church teaching, we learn that the justice of a society is tested by the treatment of the poor. The justice that was the sign of God's covenant with Israel was measured by how the poor and unprotected—the widow, the orphan, and the stranger—were treated. The kingdom that Jesus proclaimed in his word and ministry excludes no one. Throughout Israel's history and in early Christianity, the poor are agents of God's transforming power. "The Spirit of the Lord is upon me, therefore he has anointed me. He has sent me to bring glad tidings to the poor" (Lk 4:18). This was Jesus' first public utterance. Jesus takes the side of those most in need. In the Last Judgment, so dramatically described in St. Matthew's Gospel, we are told that we will be judged according to how we respond to the hungry, the thirsty, the naked, the stranger. As followers of Christ, we are challenged to make a fundamental "option for the poor"—to speak for the voiceless, to defend the defenseless, to assess life styles, policies, and social institutions in terms of their impact on the poor. This "option for the poor" does not mean pitting one group against another, but rather, strengthening the whole community by assisting those who are most vulnerable. As Christians, we are called to respond to the needs of *all* our brothers and sisters, but those with the greatest needs require the greatest response. . . .

Chronology

September 8, 1565
First Roman Catholic Mass in America celebrated, at St. Augustine, Florida

March 25, 1634
Maryland colony settled by Catholic proprietor Cecil Calvert

May 1789
John Carroll elected first Roman Catholic bishop of the United States

July 31, 1809
American Sisters of Charity founded by Elizabeth Bayley Seton

August 11, 1834
Anti-Catholic rioters set fire to Ursuline convent in Charlestown, Massachusetts

1836
Henriette Delille founds Sisters of the Holy Family, an African-American women's religious community

1845–50
Potato famine in Ireland drives 1.8 million refugees to North America

1857
St. Mary Magdalen da Pazzi, first permanent Italian-American parish, founded in Philadelphia

1858
Congregation of the Missionary Priests of St. Paul the Apostle (the Paulists) founded by Isaac Hecker

1864
St. Stanislaus Kostka Society founded by Polish immigrants in Chicago

1882
Knights of Columbus founded in New Haven, Connecticut

1891
Pope Leo XIII issues encyclical *Rerum Novarum* ("On the Condition of the Working Classes")

January 1899
Pope Leo XIII rebukes Catholic "Americanism" in papal letter *Testem Benevolentiae* ("Witness to Good Will")

1919
National Catholic Welfare Council

releases *The Bishop's Program of Social Reconstruction*

1928
Alfred E. Smith gains Democratic presidential nomination but is defeated in general election by Herbert Hoover

May 1933
Catholic Worker movement launched in New York City

1952
Monsignor Fulton J. Sheen begins weekly television program, *Life Is Worth Living*

November 1960
John F. Kennedy is elected the nation's first Roman Catholic President

1962–65
Second Vatican Council meets in Vatican City

1968
Pope Paul VI issues encyclical *Humanae Vitae* ("Of Human Life")

January 1973
U.S. Supreme Court strikes down state laws against abortion in *Roe* v. *Wade;* Catholic Church immediately takes lead in right-to-life movement

1984
Geraldine Ferraro, an Italian-American Catholic from Queens, New York, becomes the first woman to appear on a major party Presidential ticket, as running mate to Walter Mondale.

1993
Pope John Paul II, during the third of five visits to America during his pontificate, celebrates Mass for 400,000 spectators attending World Youth Day festivities in Denver, Colorado.

1999
By a vote of 223 to 31, American bishops approve a document implementing *Ex Corde Ecclesiae* ("From the Heart of the Church"), a 1990 Vatican directive on higher education. *Ex Corde Ecclesiae* called on Catholic colleges and universities to reassert their religious identity.

Further Reading

GENERAL

Ahlstrom, Sidney. *A Religious History of the American People.* New Haven, Conn.: Yale University Press, 1972.

Butler, Jon, and Harry S. Stout, eds. *Religion in American History: A Reader.* New York: Oxford University Press, 1997.

Gaustad, Edwin S. *A Religious History of America.* Revised edition. San Francisco: Harper & Row, 1990.

Marty, Martin. *Pilgrims in Their Own Land: 500 Years of Religion in America.* New York: Penguin, 1985.

GENERAL READINGS ON CATHOLICISM IN AMERICA

Butler, Jon. *Awash in a Sea of Faith: Christianizing the American People.* Cambridge, Mass.: Harvard University Press, 1990.

Carey, Patrick W. *The Roman Catholics in America.* Westport, Conn.: Praeger, 1996.

Crews, Clyde F. *American & Catholic: A Popular History of Catholicism in the United States.* Cincinnati: St. Anthony Messenger Press, 1994.

Dolan, Jay P. *The American Catholic Experience.* Garden City, N.Y.: Doubleday, 1985.

Ellis, John Tracy. *Catholics in Colonial America.* Baltimore: Helicon, 1965.

Gillis, Chester. *Roman Catholicism in America.* New York: Columbia University Press, 1999.

Glazier, Michael, and Shelley, Thomas, eds. *The Encyclopedia of American Catholic History.* Collegeville, Minn.: Liturgical Press, 1997.

Gleason, Philip. *Keeping the Faith: American Catholicism Past and Present.* Notre Dame, Ind.: University of Notre Dame Press, 1987.

Hennesey, James. *American Catholics.* New York: Oxford University Press, 1981.

Moore, R. Laurence. *Religious Outsiders and the Making of Americans.* New York: Oxford University Press, 1986.

Morris, Charles R. *American Catholic: The Saints and Sinners Who Built America's Most Powerful Church.* New York: Times Books, 1997.

CULTURAL STUDIES

Allitt, Patrick. *Catholic Converts: British and American Intellectuals Turn to Rome.* Ithaca, N.Y.: Cornell University Press, 1997.

Franchot, Jenny. *Roads to Rome: The Antebellum Protestant Encounter with Catholicism.* Berkeley: University of California Press, 1994.

Greely, Andrew M. *The Catholic Imagination.* Berkeley: University of California Press, 2000.

Massa, Mark S. *Catholics and American Culture.* New York: Oxford University Press, 1999.

DEVOTIONALISM AND SPIRITUALITY

Chinnici, Joseph P., O.F.M. *Living Stones: The History and Structure of Catholic Spiritual Life in the United States.* New York: Macmillan, 1989.

Dolan, Jay P. *Catholic Revivalism: The American Experience, 1830–1900.* Notre Dame, Ind.: University of Notre Dame Press, 1978.

O'Brien, David J. *Isaac Hecker: An American Catholic.* New York: Paulist Press, 1992.

Taves, Ann. *The Household of Faith: Roman Catholic Devotions in Mid-Nineteenth Century America.* Notre Dame, Ind.: University of Notre Dame Press, 1986.

ETHNIC AND COMMUNITY STUDIES

Burns, Jeffrey M. *San Francisco: A History of the Archdiocese of San Francisco.* Vol. 1. *1776–1884: From Mission to Golden Frontier.* Strasbourg, France: Editions du Signe, 1999.

Davis, Cyprian. *The History of Black Catholics in the United States.* New York: Crossroad, 1991.

Kane, Paula M. *Separatism and Subculture: Boston Catholicism, 1900–1920.* Chapel Hill: University of North Carolina Press, 1994.

Matovina, Timothy M. *Tejano Religion and Ethnicity.* Austin: University of Texas Press, 1995.

Miller, Kerby. *Emigrants and Exiles: Ireland and the Irish Exodus to North America.* New York: Oxford University Press, 1985.

Miller, Randall M., and Wakelyn, Jon, eds. *Catholics in the Old South: Essays on Church and Culture.* Macon, Ga.: Mercer University Press, 1983.

Orsi, Robert A. *The Madonna of 115th Street: Faith and Community in Italian Harlem, 1880–1950.* New Haven, Conn.: Yale University Press, 1985.

Parot, Joseph J. *Polish Catholics in Chicago, 1850–1920: A Religious History.* De Kalb, Ill.: Northern Illinois University Press, 1981.

Sandoval, Moises. *On the Move: A History of the Hispanic Church in the United States.* Maryknoll, New York: Orbis Books, 1990.

Skerrett, Ellen, ed. *At the Crossroads: Old Saint Patrick's and the Chicago Irish.* Chicago: Wild Onion Books, 1997.

Tweed, Thomas A. *Our Lady of the Exile. Diasporic Religion at a Cuban Shrine in Miami.* New York: Oxford University Press, 1997.

Vecsey, Christopher. *American Indian Catholics. Vol. 1. On the Padres' Trail.* Notre Dame, Ind.: University of Notre Dame Press, 1996.

HISTORIES OF CATHOLIC WOMEN

Coburn, Carol, and Smith, Martha. *Spirited Lives: How Nuns Shaped Catholic Culture and American Life, 1836-1920.* Chapel Hill: University of North Carolina Press, 1999.

Ewens, Mary. *The Role of the Nun in Nineteenth-Century America.* Salem, N.H.: Ayer, 1984.

Kenneally, James J. *The History of American Catholic Women.* New York: Crossroad, 1990.

Kennelly, Karen, ed. *American Catholic Women: A Historical Exploration.* New York: Macmillan, 1989.

PERSONAL NARRATIVES

Cabeza de Vaca. *Journey to the Unknown Interior of America.* Translated and edited by Cyclone Covey. Albuquerque: University of New Mexico Press, 1961.

Day, Dorothy. *The Long Loneliness: An Autobiography.* New York: Harper & Row, 1952.

McCarthy, Abigail. *Private Faces/Public Places.* Garden City, N.Y.: Doubleday, 1972.

Rodriguez, Richard. *Days of Obligation: An Argument with My Mexican Father.* New York: Penguin, 1993.

POLITICS AND SOCIAL ACTION

Allitt, Patrick. *Catholic Intellectuals and Conservative Politics in America, 1950–1985.* Ithaca, N.Y.: Cornell University Press, 1993.

Kauffman, Christopher J. *Faith and Fraternalism: The History of the Knights of Columbus.* New York: Simon & Schuster, 1992.

McGreevy, John T. *Parish Boundaries: The Catholic Encounter with Race in the Twentieth-Century Urban North.* Chicago: University of Chicago Press, 1996.

Meconis, Charles A. *With Clumsy Grace: The American Catholic Left, 1961–1975.* New York: Seabury Press, 1979.

O'Brien, David J. *Public Catholicism.* New York: Macmillan, 1989.

Polner, Murray, and O'Grady, Jim. *Disarmed and Dangerous: The Radical Lives and Times of Daniel and Philip Berrigan.* New York: Basic Books, 1997.

REFERENCE WORKS AND DOCUMENT COLLECTIONS

Abell, Aaron I. *American Catholic Thought on Social Questions.* Indianapolis: Bobbs-Merrill, 1968.

Catechism of the Catholic Church. Liguori, Mo.: Liguori Publications, 1994.

Ellis, John Tracy. *Documents of American Catholic History.* 3 vols. Wilmington, Del.: Michael Glazier, 1987.

Flannery, Austin, ed. *Vatican Council II: The Conciliar and Post Conciliar Documents.* Northport, N.Y.: Costello Publishing Co., 1975.

Glazier, Michael, and Shelley, Thomas, eds. *The Encyclopedia of American Catholic History.* Collegeville, Minn.: Liturgical Press, 1997.

McBrien, Richard P., ed. *The HarperCollins Encyclopedia of Catholicism.* New York: HarperCollins, 1995.

Index

Acknowledgments

I am deeply grateful to Mark Reynolds for his expert research assistance in the preparation of this book. For their advice and suggestions I also wish to thank Jeffrey M. Burns and Roy P. Domenico, two fine gentlemen and scholars in the American Catholic tradition. Like every student of American Catholic history, I am indebted to the work of Christopher J. Kauffman, editor of *U.S. Catholic Historian*, an indispensable journal that has transformed our field.

Picture Credits

American Antiquarian Society: 36; Courtesy of the Arizona Historical Society/Tucson (AHS # 62996): 83; Diocese of Belleville, Illinois: 31; Boston Public Library: 81; Catholic News Service: 2, 122, 127, 140, 148, 150, 159; Archives of the Catholic University of America, NCWC/Social Action Department: 101; Champlain Society: 20–21; Chicago Historical Society: 40; Corbis: 26, 144; artist Ralph Fasanella, courtesy of ACA Galleries: cover; Florida State Archives: 10, 14, 15, 16; Georgetown University Library: 117; Grailville Archive: 121; Holy Cross Church, Kentucky: 41; Hunter College Archives: 143; Josephite Fathers Archives: 123; John F. Kennedy Library: 118, 135; Courtesy of the Knights of Columbus Headquarters Museum: 103; Courtesy of the Knights of Columbus/Photo Archive: 89, 125, 131; Library of Congress: 22, 47, 55, 92, 93, 71, 85, 90, 104, 110; Los Angeles Public Library/Shades of L.A. Archives: 157; Marquette University: 111, 115; Photography Collections, University of Maryland, Baltimore County: 35, 39; Permission of the Merton Legacy Trust: 129; Richter Library of the University of Miami: 155; Courtesy of the Archives of the Archdiocese of Milwaukee: 29; Minnesota Historical Society: 6; Museum of Modern Art, Film Stills: 130; National Portrait Gallery, Smithsonian Institution/Art Resource, NY: 32; Courtesy of the Museum of New Mexico, (Neg. No. 5524) 13, (Neg. No. 14409) 17; © Collection of The New York Historical Society: 57, 61, 65; New York Public Library, Rare Books: 54; Notre Dame Archives: 7, 64, 86, 98, 128; Flannery O'Connor Collection, Ina Dillard Russell Library, Georgia College and State University: 133; Paulist History Archives: 74; Poor Clare Monastery of Our Lady of Guadalupe, Roswell, New Mexico: 154; Queens Borough Public Library, Long Island Division, Herald Tribune Photo Morgue: 147; Ricco/Maresca Gallery/Art Resource: 28; Franklin D. Roosevelt Library: 108; Saint Louis University Archives: 46; Sisters of the Holy Family Motherhouse and Novitiate: 60; Sisters of Mercy: 163; Society for the Preservation of New England Antiquities: 50; Society of the Sacred Heart National Archive: 45; The UT Institute of Texan Cultures at San Antonio: 59 (Courtesy of Dr. M. W. Sharp), 76 (Courtesy of Mr. Joe Kotch, Sr.), 78 (No. 82-139), 84 (The San Antonio Light Collection); State Historical Society of Wisconsin: 106

Text Credits

"Jacques Marquette's Journey Down the Mississippi River," p. 24. Reuben Gold Thwaites, ed. *The Jesuit Relations and Allied Documents: Travels and Explorations of the Jesuit Missionaries in New France, 1610–1791.* Vol. LIX: *Lower Canada, Illinois, Ottawas* (Cleveland: Burrows Brothers, 1900), pp. 161, 163.

"Frontier Sisters," p. 42–43. Margory Erskine, *Mother Philippine Duchesne* (New York: Longmans, Green, 1926), pp. 196–98.

"Isaac Hecker on the Eucharist," p. 74–75. Isaac Hecker, *Questions of the Soul* (New York: Catholic Publication House, 1855), pp. 207–209.

"Mr. Dooley on Lent," p. 94–95. *Dissertations by Mr. Dooley* (New York: Harper & Brothers, 1906), 123–26.

"The Inaugural Issue of the Catholic Worker," p. 112–113. *The Catholic Worker*, Vol. 1, No. 1 (May 1933).

"John F. Kennedy Confronts the Religion Issue," p. 138–139. John F. Kennedy, Speech Before Greater Houston Ministerial Association, September 12, 1960.

"The American Bishops Speak Out on Economic Injustice," p. 164–165. *Economic Justice for All*, Pastoral Letter on Catholic Social Teaching and the United States Economy (Washington, D.C.: United States Catholic Conference, 1986).

James T. Fisher

James T. Fisher holds the Danforth Chair in Humanities at Saint Louis University, where he is also Professor of History and Theological Studies. He is the author of *The Catholic Counterculture in America, 1933–1962* and *Dr. America, the Lives of Thomas A. Dooley, 1927–1961*. As a faculty fellow of the Delta Teachers Academy, Professor Fisher has worked with secondary school teachers seeking to integrate American religious history into programs in the humanities. He holds a Ph.D. from Rutgers University and previously taught in the American Studies program at Yale University.

Jon Butler

Jon Butler is the William Robertson Coe Professor of American Studies and History and Professor of Religious Studies at Yale University. He received his B.A. and Ph.D. in history from the University of Minnesota. He is the coauthor, with Harry S. Stout, of *Religion in American History: A Reader*, and the author of several other books in American religious history including *Awash in a Sea of Faith: Christianizing the American People*, which won the Beveridge Award for the best book in American history in 1990 from the American Historical Association.

Harry S. Stout

Harry S. Stout is the Jonathan Edwards Professor of American Christianity at Yale University. He is the general editor of the Religion in America series for Oxford University Press and co-editor of *Readings in American Religious History, New Directions in American Religious History, A Jonathan Edwards Reader*, and *The Dictionary of Christianity in America*. His book *The Divine Dramatist: George Whitefield and the Rise of Modern Evangelicalism* was nominated for a Pulitzer Prize in 1991.